The Trial
of Galileo
Science Versus the Inquisition

The Trial
of Galileo
Science Versus the Inquisition

Other books in the Famous Trials series:

The Trial of Galileo
Science Versus the Inquisition

by Don Nardo

FAMOUS
TRIALS

LUCENT
BOOKS®

THOMSON
™
GALE

San Diego • Detroit • New York • San Francisco • Cleveland
New Haven, Conn. • Waterville, Maine • London • Munich

THOMSON
━━━━━━━✦━━━━━━━ ™
GALE

LIBRARY OF CONGRESS CATALOGING-IN-PUBLICATION DATA

Nardo, Don, 1947–
  The trial of Galileo : science versus the Inquisition / by Don Nardo.
    p. cm. — (Famous trials)
  Includes bibliographical references and index.
  Contents: An outspoken thinker in an age of change — The new astronomy vs. the Holy
Scriptures — Galileo on trial : the initial depositions — Galileo on trial : the sentence and
abjuration — The legacy of Galileo and his trial.
  ISBN 1-59018-423-8 (lib. bdg. : alk. paper)
  1. Galilei, Galileo, 1564–1642—Juvenile literature. 2. Galilei, Galileo, 1564–1642—Trials,
litigation, etc.—Juvenile literature. 3. Trials (Heresy)—Italy—Rome—Juvenile literature.
4. Inquisition—Italy—Rome—Juvenile literature. 5. Astronomers—Italy—Biography—
Juvenile literature. [1. Galileo, 1564–1642. 2. Galileo, 1564–1642—Trials, litigation, etc.
3. Trials (Heresy) 4. Inquisition—Italy. 5. Astronomers. 6. Scientists.] I. Title. II. Series.
  QB36.G2N37 2004
  520'.92—dc22

                                                                                2003026299

Printed in the United States of America

Table of Contents

Foreword

"The law is not an end in and of itself, nor does it provide ends. It is preeminently a means to serve what we think is right."

William J. Brennan Jr.

THE CONCEPT OF JUSTICE AND THE RULE OF LAW are hallmarks of Western civilization, manifested perhaps most visibly in widely famous and dramatic court trials. These trials include such important and memorable personages as the ancient Greek philosopher Socrates, who was accused and convicted of corrupting the minds of his society's youth in 399 B.C.; the French maiden and military leader Joan of Arc, accused and convicted of heresy against the church in 1431; to former football star O.J. Simpson, acquitted of double murder in 1995. These and other well-known and controversial trials constitute the most public, and therefore most familiar, demonstrations of a Western legal tradition that dates back through the ages. Although no one is certain when the first law code appeared or when the first formal court trials were held, Babylonian ruler Hammurabi introduced the first known law code in about 1760 B.C. It remains unclear how this code was administered, and no records of specific trials have survived. What is clear, however, is that humans have always sought to govern behavior and define actions in terms of law.

Almost all societies have made laws and prosecuted people for going against those laws, but the question of which behaviors to sanction and which to censure has always been controversial and remains in flux. Some, such as Roman orator and legislator Cicero, argue that laws are simply applications of universal standards. Cicero believed that humanity would agree on what constituted illegal behavior and that human laws were a mere extension of natural laws. "True law is right reason in agreement with nature," he wrote, world-wide in scope, unchanging, everlasting. . . . We may not oppose or alter that law, we cannot abolish it, we cannot be freed from its obligations by any legislature. . . . This [natural] law does not differ for Rome and for Athens, for the present and for the future. . . . It is and will be valid for all nations and all times.

Cicero's rather optimistic view has been contradicted throughout history, however. For every law made to preserve harmony and set universal standards of behavior, another has been born of fear, prejudice, greed, desire for power, and a host of other motives. History is replete with individuals defying and fighting to change such laws—and even to topple governments that dictate such laws. Abolitionists fought against slavery, civil rights leaders fought for equal rights, millions throughout the world have fought for independence—these constitute a minimum of reasons for which people have sought to overturn laws that they believed to be wrong or unjust. In opposition to Cicero, then, many others, such as eighteenth-century English poet and philosopher William Godwin, believe humans must be constantly vigilant against bad laws. As Godwin said in 1793:

Laws we sometimes call the wisdom of our ancestors. But this is a strange imposition. It was as frequently the dictate of their passion, of timidity, jealousy, a monopolizing spirit, and a lust of power that knew no bounds. Are we not obliged perpetually to renew and remodel this misnamed wisdom of our ancestors? To correct it by a detection of their ignorance, and a censure of their intolerance?

Lucent Books' *Famous Trials* series showcases trials that exemplify both society's praiseworthy condemnation of universally unacceptable behavior, and its misguided persecution of individuals based on fear and ignorance, as well as trials that leave open the question of whether justice has been done. Each volume begins by setting the scene and providing a historical context to show how society's mores influence the trial process and the verdict.

Each book goes on to present a detailed and lively account of the trial, including liberal use of primary source material such as direct testimony, lawyers' summations, and contemporary and modern commentary. In addition, sidebars throughout the text create a broader context by presenting illuminating details about important points of law, information on key personalities, and important distinctions related to civil, federal, and criminal procedures. Thus, all of the primary and secondary source material included in both the text and the sidebars demonstrates to readers the sources and methods historians use to derive information and conclusions about such events.

Lastly, each *Famous Trials* volume includes one or more of the following comprehensive tools that motivate readers to pursue further reading and research. A timeline allows readers to see the scope of the trial at a glance, annotated bibliographies provide both sources for further research and a thorough list of works consulted, a glossary helps students with unfamiliar words and concepts, and a comprehensive index permits quick scanning of the book as a whole.

The insight of Oliver Wendell Holmes Jr., distinguished Supreme Court justice, exemplifies the theme of the *Famous Trials* series. Taken from *The Common Law*, published in 1881, Holmes remarked: "The life of the law has not been logic, it has been experience." That "experience" consists mainly in how laws are applied in society and challenged in the courts, a process resulting in differing outcomes from one generation to the next. Thus, the *Famous Trials* series encourages readers to examine trials within a broader historical and social context.

Introduction

When Religion and Science Work at Cross-Purposes

O N JUNE 22, 1633, a sixty-nine-year-old man named Galileo Galilei knelt before a group of leading churchmen in Rome and declared that he did not believe that Earth moved around the Sun. Furthermore, the Sun did not lie at the center of the known universe, as he had earlier advocated. "I must altogether abandon the false opinion that the Sun is the center of the world and immovable," he stated,

> and that the Earth is not the center of the world, and moves.
> ... With sincere heart and unfeigned faith I abjure [renounce],
> curse, and detest the . . . errors and heresies [I have com-
> mitted] and . . . I swear that in the future I will never again
> say or assert, verbally or in writing, anything that might fur-
> nish occasion for a similar suspicion regarding me. [1]

This formal abjuration (renouncement or denial) of his former principles was an astonishing reversal for Galileo. In a remark-
able career, he had made important contributions to early modern science, including experiments that revealed some of nature's
laws of motion. In the discipline of astronomy, he had been the
first person to apply a new invention, the telescope, to studies of
the heavens; in short order, he had discovered craters and mountains on the Moon, the phases of the planet Venus, the existence

11

Pictured is Galileo's room in Florence, Italy, carefully preserved by the Italian government. The chamber still contains some of his astronomical instruments.

of sunspots, and the four largest moons of Jupiter. In addition, he had championed the heliocentric (Sun-centered) view of the universe, which Polish astronomer Nicolaus Copernicus had introduced in the 1540s.

Considering these achievements, it might seem strange that Galileo would suddenly renounce his belief in the heliocentric system. But in fact, he was given no choice in the matter. In his zeal to promote new scientific ideas, he came up against the Roman Catholic Church, which steadfastly held that Earth rested motionless at the center of all things. Members of the Inquisition (a group of priests charged with suppressing antireligious views) claimed that churchmen had in the past warned Galileo not to advocate such ideas. And when he continued to do so, the Inquisition brought him to trial. Galileo's abjuration of his belief in the Copernican system was part of the punishment meted out in his sentence.

Science vs. Scripture

Nearly four centuries have elapsed since Galileo's trial. Yet interest in it and how it came about remains strong. Indeed, as Jerome J. Langford, one of the leading modern scholars of the trial, puts it, "The question of Galileo and the Roman Catholic Church seems destined never to die out." [2] This continuing interest in Galileo's confrontation with the church is undoubtedly due in large part to the dramatic nature of the events involved, as well as to later perceptions of Galileo as a larger-than-life character. These factors, says Richard Blackwell of St. Louis University,

> continue to attract the attention of the scholar, the novelist, and the playwright. Images easily multiply of the flawed tragic hero, of the struggle for intellectual freedom, of the unprotected individual pitted against a powerful institution committed to its self-preservation, and of the plots and subplots and counterplots worthy of the best mystery writer. [3]

Thus, in many modern accounts Galileo has been portrayed as a great genius and courageous martyr who stood up to the backward-thinking, antiscientific, and corrupt church; as a result, he suffered horrible persecution.

This scenario is somewhat exaggerated and misleading. There is no doubt that the church's position regarding Earth and the Sun was wrong; after all, Earth does revolve around the Sun and not the other way around. Also, the pope and the Inquisition committed a grave error and did Galileo a great disservice by putting him on trial, forcing him to recant his views, and imprisoning him.

Yet to say that the church did these things because it was corrupt and against science is inaccurate, mainly because it uses too simplistic a brush to paint what was in reality a much more complex picture. First, few of the clergymen in Galileo's day were hostile toward science or the advancement of human knowledge. In fact, the church often supported scientific endeavors, and a number of priests were mathematicians and astronomers. The problem, at least from a modern standpoint, was that, at the time, science was not defined or thought of as it is today. Science was still largely part of philosophy, a branch of learning in which ideas are discussed and debated without the need for compelling proof to back them up. Often, scholars gave credence to theories with no real scientific merit as long as they were well argued and interesting.

Furthermore, science was expected to bow its head to religion. Most people in Europe in those days were highly devout Christians who viewed the Scriptures (the texts making up the Bible) and the church itself as the ultimate sources of truth. Worldly affairs and ideas, including scientific ones, were seen as less authoritative and prestigious than religious doctrine. Therefore, the intent of leading churchmen was not to impede scientific progress or stifle the truth. Rather, they wanted to ensure that what they sincerely believed was the truth, as revealed in the Scriptures, was not distorted by misguided scientific notions. After all, in their worldview, scientists were human and therefore subject to error, whereas the Scriptures represented God's word and were therefore infallible.

Under these intellectual conditions, most churchmen strongly backed and even revered scientists whose ideas conformed with the descriptions of the heavens in the Scriptures. The ancient Greek scientists Aristotle and Ptolemy were widely seen as almost infallible sages, for example. This was because their writings supported the geocentric (Earth-centered) concept of the heavens that the Scriptures appeared to advocate. So when men like Galileo challenged the traditional view, they appeared to threaten the integrity of divine truth and the very foundations of the social order that the church had worked so hard to cultivate. The clergymen who opposed Galileo, noted scholar Charles Van Doren writes,

> deeply believed in the Ptolemaic system and the Aristotelian world order, but not because they were physicists who thought that those theories better explained the phenomena. They believed in the old theories because the theories supported even more deeply held beliefs. And to question those deepest beliefs was to bring their world crashing down around their heads. They could not face that possibility. [4]

Galileo (holding the map) stands before members of the Inquisition in June 1633 shortly before renouncing the heliocentric view of the universe.

The Creation of a Martyr

As for Galileo himself, in some ways he was undeniably a victim of the irrational fears of some of the leading churchmen of his time. His trial was a misguided attempt to silence him, and his sentence of abjuration and imprisonment was, by modern standards, overly harsh, cruel, and counterproductive to the free exchange of ideas. But to describe Galileo as a courageous martyr who stood up to the church and valiantly defended his views is to deny the facts. Over the course of more than twenty years, he repeatedly tried to appease religious authorities for fear of being punished. Often he tried to couch his scientific writings in formats that made them look like they were not formally advocating Copernican ideas. And when the church finally brought him to trial, he wasted no time in offering to refute the heliocentric view, in writing if necessary.

In fact, the image of Galileo as a great martyr of science, which is largely a myth, did not materialize until after his death. Instrumental in the creation of this image was one of his former students, Vincenzo Viviani, whose *Life of Galileo* was published posthumously in 1717. Viviani idolized his former teacher and friend. And the biography contains numerous invented episodes and other embellishments designed to make Galileo seem almost divinely or magically inspired in his efforts to revolutionize humanity's views of the universe. Many later writers accepted some of these distortions without question and further amplified the scientist's legend. Moreover, the more heroic Galileo became, the more despicable those who put him on trial seemed in contrast. In a Galileo biography published in 1793, for instance, Italian historian Giovanni de' Nelli stated:

> It is amazing to see the extent of the friars' hatred and the attitude of the Pontiff [Pope] to his divine author. . . . The Pope, the Inquisition, the friars . . . with the utmost extravagance found unheard-of ways to torment the spirit of that unfortunate philosopher.[5]

In truth, most leading churchmen did not hate Galileo, nor did they torment him, either during or after his trial. Though some of

Vincenzo Viviani, Galileo's student and companion, wrote a biography of the scientist that greatly exaggerated his abilities and achievements.

his inquisitors were stern with him, all were civil and a few were quite sympathetic to both his ideas and his plight and worked hard to acquit him. Also, the church made sure he was comfortable during the trial and he was never jailed or physically hurt in any way. Indeed, after the trial Galileo was allowed to serve out his "prison"

term first in the lavish villa of an archbishop who admired him greatly and later in the comfort of his own home.

Furthermore, Galileo must himself bear at least some of the blame for his misfortune. The evidence suggests that he was overly optimistic about how quickly the religious and intellectual establishment would accept an entirely new and jarring conception of Earth and its place in the universe. He evidently sincerely believed that all that was needed was for the authorities to peer through the lens of a telescope, as he had. Surely, they would then be convinced and embrace the new astronomy. Yet the reality was that few of these men were ready to accept anything that might make them doubt the literal truth of the Scriptures, even evidence viewed through their own eyes. So when Galileo, moved by his scientific enthusiasm, pushed them too hard, they pushed back. In Langford's words:

> [Galileo] was a man of his times, and whether he liked it or not, he should at least have recognized the fact that mankind was not about to accept, on his word alone, an entirely new view of the universe. . . . Man liked to think that all creation revolved around him, that the heavens surrounding him were put there . . . for his enjoyment. Too much was against him. Not just physics, not merely fundamentalist [religious doctrine], but centuries of acceptance by everyone, or nearly everyone, that the Sun really moved and the Earth did not.[6]

Thus, Galileo's run-in with the church, which culminated in his trial, was not about a heroic scientist confronting an ignorant and corrupt establishment; it was more about religion and science working at cross-purposes, with sad and destructive results for both. Each side misjudged the other, made tragic mistakes, and paid a heavy price. Galileo was humiliated and lost his freedom, while the church gained a worse reputation for

This statue of Galileo stands in Florence, one of the cities in which he lived and worked. Italians view Galileo as one of their greatest heroes.

intolerance toward science and progress than it actually deserved. Indeed, in the eyes of some people the church has still not erased its guilt in the Galileo affair. Although the church long ago gave in and recognized the truth of the Copernican system, the struggle between Christian religion and science continues to this day on other fronts (evolution, abortion, cloning, and so forth). For that reason, some of the core issues surrounding Galileo's trial are still relevant and are likely to remain so for a long time to come.

Chapter 1

An Outspoken Thinker in an Age of Change

IN RETROSPECT, GALILEO'S dispute with the church and the trial that grew out of that disagreement were not surprising developments for the era in which they occurred. Galileo Galilei was born in the northern Italian town of Pisa on February 15, 1564. The years immediately preceding and directly following his birth were "a time of discovery and rediscovery, of rapid change and anxiety,"[7] Jerome Langford points out. Indeed, momentous currents of change were sweeping through medieval Europe, altering the way people viewed the world, society, and long-cherished institutions and beliefs.

One of the most irresistible of these currents of change was the sudden and rapid expansion of Europe's physical, political, and economic horizons. In the late 1400s and early 1500s, European explorers discovered North and South America. And in 1522, ships from the expedition of Spain's Ferdinand Magellan returned from the first voyage around the globe. Each succeeding year witnessed the opening of new trade routes into the Americas in the West, and India, China, and other Asian lands in the East. All the while European manufacturers and noblemen grew rich, while the courts of their kings became more splendid and powerful than ever before.

The growing wealth and authority of the kings and nobles helped to drive another fateful current that swept European society during the age into which Galileo was born. The Roman

Catholic Church had been Europe's most powerful and influential institution for a thousand years. During the medieval centuries, the pope and other church leaders based in Rome had almost completely dominated European society. They had dictated what behavior was moral and acceptable, basing their teachings mostly on passages in the Bible. But as Europe's kings grew more powerful in the age of exploration, they began to challenge the church's authority. Monarchs in France and Spain began appointing their own bishops. And in the 1520s, German clergyman Martin Luther, who preached that church authorities in Rome had grown too powerful and corrupt, spearheaded the Reformation. Those who agreed with Luther became known as Protestants and broke away from the Catholic Church. Another split with Rome occurred in 1533, only a few decades before Galileo was born. When the pope refused to grant Henry VIII, king of England, a divorce, Henry abandoned Catholicism and formed the Church of England.

Thus, Galileo entered a world in which the church's authority had begun to erode. Catholic leaders feared not only for themselves but also for society, which they believed would be damaged by the ongoing assault on religious tradition. "Then as now, there were longstanding traditions which could not be ignored even though they were bound to be overcome," says Langford. "Some who lived in the age of Galileo feared . . . change as an evil and true freedom [of thought and expression] as a catastrophe."[8] Seeing themselves as defenders of righteous tradition, these conservative, fearful individuals felt it was their duty to maintain the church's authority. And they were always on the watch for anyone who advocated ideas that might, in their view, undermine that authority. Sooner or later, any outspoken thinker, as Galileo was destined to become, was bound to clash with these men; it was simply an unavoidable hazard of that turbulent age.

Galileo's Education

Actually, if Galileo's father, Vincenzio Galilei, had had his way, the young man would never have become a famous mathematician and scientist. Vincenzio hailed from a well-to-do family in Florence,

A romanticized depiction of German clergyman Martin Luther, who helped bring about the Reformation, a movement that eroded the Catholic Church's authority.

located about fifty miles northeast of Pisa. (These two cities, along with Siena, to the south, were the leading centers of Tuscany, one of several nation-states that occupied what is now the country of Italy. North of Tuscany stretched the state of Milan, and east of Milan was the Republic of Venice. Meanwhile, central Italy was dominated by the Papal States, with Rome as their capital and the pope

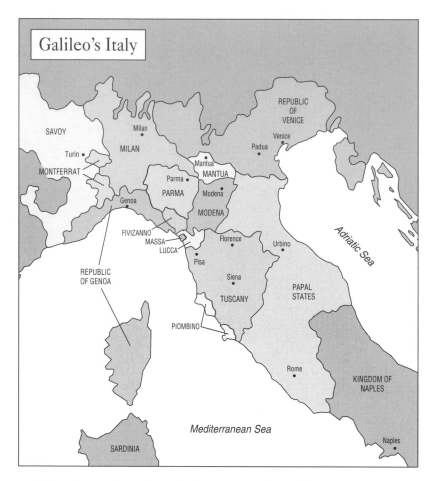

Galileo's Italy

as their ruler, and southern Italy was part of the Kingdom of Naples, then administered by Spain.) However, after becoming a musician and music teacher in Pisa, Vincenzio was able to earn only a modest living. He and his wife, Giulia, whom he married in 1562, found it hard to make ends meet, so he felt strongly that his first-born son, Galileo, should not make the same mistake he had. Instead of becoming a musician, teacher, or scholar, professions that paid little, the boy should become a doctor, Vincenzio insisted. Medicine was then one of the three most prestigious professions (along with theology and law), and its members made a lot of money.

Vincenzio's plan was to make sure that his son got a good fundamental education and then enroll him in medical school. By

1574, when Galileo was ten, the family was back in Florence and the boy was enrolled in a school in a nearby monastery. There he studied Latin and Greek, read the works of the ancient classical (Greco-Roman) writers, and learned to draw and play the lute (a guitarlike instrument). The young Galileo apparently liked the quiet life of the monastery and soon became a novice monk.

Vincenzio Galilei was not about to let his son become a penniless friar, however. When Galileo was fifteen, his father removed him from the monastery and two years later enrolled him in the highly respected school of medicine at the University of Pisa. The problem was that the young man did not want to become a doctor. At school, safely away from his father, Galileo neglected his medical studies and devoted nearly all of his attention to a new passion—mathematics. The young man became friendly with Ostillio Ricci, mathematician to the grand duke of Tuscany. And Ricci introduced him to the geometry of the ancient Greek master Euclid, as well as to the works of another long-dead Greek, the mathematician and mechanical genius Archimedes.

Eventually, Vincenzio found out what his son was up to. The furious father traveled to Pisa to demand that Galileo return to his medical studies, but Ricci intervened and convinced Vincenzio that the boy's real talent lay in mathematics. Reluctantly, Vincenzio agreed to allow Galileo to stay in school for another year. Because he had neglected his studies for so long, however, the young man could not graduate and left the university in 1585 without a degree.

Doubts About Aristotle

For the next few years, Galileo scratched out whatever small living he could tutoring young people in mathematics. Eventually, a Tuscan nobleman and a leading priest-mathematician in Rome met Galileo and were impressed by his brilliance. They used their influence to get him appointed as a mathematics professor at the University of Pisa in 1589, only four years after he had failed to graduate from the school.

Because his teaching duties were light at first, Galileo was able to devote considerable time to studying the ideas of Archimedes and determining how to apply them in new ways. In fact, one of

Archimedes' principal discoveries became instrumental in Galileo's studies of moving bodies. The ancient Greek had shown why objects are buoyant (float) in water and other fluids: Namely, such an object displaces a weight of fluid equal to its own weight. One of the ideas that Galileo was expected to teach was Aristotle's maxim that objects of different weights fall at different rates, the heavier ones falling faster than the lighter ones. However, Galileo suspected that Aristotle was wrong. It seemed to Galileo that any differences in the rates of falling bodies were the result of the buoyancy of the air. "Galileo was thus extending Archimedes' ideas about the buoyancy of water," scholar James MacLachlan points out.

> According to Archimedes, water supports objects made of materials less dense than water. Galileo reasoned that air, too, provides some support for objects of small density. So he said that less dense objects would fall more slowly in air than denser ones. Density, not weight, was the controlling factor. Galileo even went so far as to claim that if there was no air, all objects would fall at the same rate.[9]

To test this theory, Galileo simultaneously dropped two objects of different weights from the same height and watched closely as they struck the ground. (Many modern scholars think the familiar tale that he dropped these weights from the top of the Leaning Tower of Pisa is a later fabrication.) Every time he repeated the experiment, varying the weights in each instance, both objects touched the ground at the same or almost the same time. He ascribed the occasional slight differences to air resistance.

Embracing Copernicus

Thanks to these experiments, Galileo increasingly came to doubt Aristotle's ideas about motion and sometimes spoke out against them at the university. This did not go over well with his fellow academics and supervisors, who, following custom, revered Aristotle. Not surprisingly, therefore, when the young man's contract came up for renewal at the end of his third year of teaching, the university did not renew it.

The bell platform atop the Tower of Pisa. The two stone balls are replicas of those Galileo used in some of his experiments with falling weights.

Fortunately for Galileo, he soon managed to find another teaching position, this one at the University of Padua, in the Republic of Venice, in December 1592. As he had in Pisa, he taught mathematics. But his contract at Padua also called for him to teach astronomy. One of the standard textbooks he had to use was the

Sphere, written in 1240, which summarized Aristotle's views on the structure and workings of the universe. Like most other ancient Greek scholars, Aristotle held that Earth is spherical in shape and rests at the center of the universe. As proof of this, he pointed out that falling objects always move toward the center of Earth. The second piece of proof he offered was that Earth casts a curved shadow onto the Moon during lunar eclipses. In his treatise *On the Heavens*, Aristotle wrote:

> As it is, the shapes which the Moon itself each month shows are of every kind . . . but in eclipses the outline is always curved. And, since it is the interposition of the Earth [between the Sun and Moon] that makes the eclipse, the

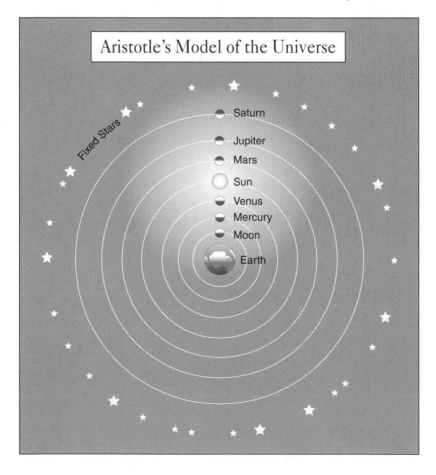

Aristotle's Model of the Universe

Fixed Stars

Saturn
Jupiter
Mars
Sun
Venus
Mercury
Moon
Earth

COPERNICUS'S RELUCTANCE TO PUBLISH

In the preface to his masterwork *On the Revolutions*, Nicolaus Copernicus addressed Pope Paul III and admitted that he had reservations about publishing his controversial theory that Earth moves around the Sun.

> I can readily imagine, Holy Father, that as soon as some people hear that in this volume, which I have written about the revolutions of the spheres of the universe, I ascribe certain motions to the terrestrial globe [i.e., Earth], they will shout that I must be immediately repudiated together with this belief. . . . Those who know that the consensus of many centuries has sanctioned the conception that the Earth remains at rest in the middle of the heaven as its center would, I reflected, regard it as an insane pronouncement if I made the opposite assertion that the Earth moves. Therefore I debated with myself for a long time whether to publish the volume which I wrote to prove the Earth's motion. . . . When I weighed these considerations, the scorn which I had reason to fear on account of the novelty and unconventionality of my opinion almost induced me to abandon completely the work which I had undertaken.

form of this line will be caused by the form of the Earth's surface, which is therefore spherical.[10]

This much—that Earth is a sphere—Galileo and other scholars of his day, including churchmen, agreed on. (Most people did not think that Earth was flat, as commonly portrayed in modern times.) But Galileo came to believe that Aristotle was wrong about the way he pictured the overall structure of the cosmos. In this picture, the heavens consisted of a series of large, invisible spheres that were concentric, or nested within one another. Each sphere supposedly held in place a planet or other celestial body and accounted for a specific visible motion in the sky. Thus, the Sun rested on one sphere, Mars was attached to a larger sphere beyond, Jupiter was on still another and more distant sphere, and so forth.

But if Earth was motionless at the center of these celestial spheres, Galileo reasoned, what caused the oceans to produce tides? It seemed to him that the tides would be better explained if Earth was moving (since such movement might jostle the oceans, making waves, an idea later proved to be wrong). And this led him to closer

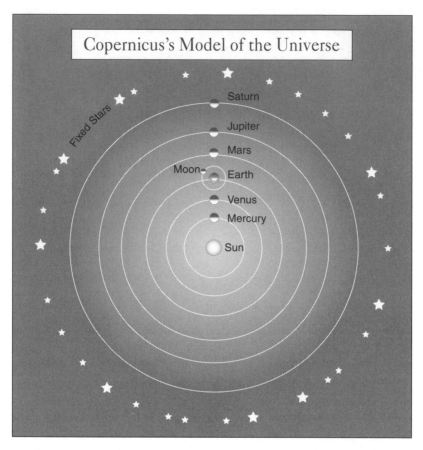

examine the heliocentric model of the heavens that Nicolaus Copernicus had proposed in 1543 (which was still widely viewed only as a theory). According to Copernicus in his *On the Revolutions:*

> The Sun is the center of the universe. Moreover, since the Sun remains stationary, whatever appears as a motion of the Sun is really due rather to the motion of the Earth. In comparison with any other spheres of the planets, the distance from the Earth to the Sun has a magnitude which is quite appreciable in proportion to those dimensions. But the size of the universe is so great that the distance Earth-Sun is imperceptible in relation to the sphere of the fixed stars. This should be admitted, I believe, in preference to perplexing the mind with an almost infinite multitude of spheres, as

must be done by those who kept the Earth in the middle of the universe. [11]

Galileo wanted to publish a book supporting the Copernican theory, as well as teach that theory in his classes. But most scientists, especially church astronomers, had ridiculed Copernicus, which made Galileo think twice. In 1597 he wrote to the great German astronomer Johannes Kepler. Kepler also embraced the heliocentric system, and Galileo valued his opinion about whether or not to publish. Galileo wrote:

Like you, I accepted the Copernican position several years ago and discovered from thence the causes of many natural effects which are doubtless inexplicable by the current theories. I have written up many of my reasons and refutations on the subject, but I have not dared until now to bring them into the open, being warned by the fortunes

KEPLER URGES GALILEO TO GO PUBLIC

Galileo wrote to German astronomer Johannes Kepler in 1597 and indicated that the time did not yet seem right to express public support for the Copernican theory. Kepler's reply, excerpted here from volume 10 of *Le Opere di Galileo Galilei,* urged Galileo to take a bolder approach.

I could only have wished that you, who have so profound an insight, would choose another way. You advise us, by your personal example, and in discreetly veiled fashion, to retreat before the general ignorance and not to expose ourselves or heedlessly to oppose the violent attacks of the mob of scholars. . . . Would it not be much better to pull the wagon to its goal by our joint efforts, now that we have got it under way, and gradually, with powerful voices, to shout down the common herd, which really does not weigh the arguments very carefully? Thus perhaps by cleverness we may bring it to a knowledge of the truth. . . . Be of good cheer, Galileo, and come out publicly. If I judge correctly, there are only a few of the distinguished mathematicians of Europe who would part company with us, so great is the power of truth. If Italy seems a less favorable place for your publication, and if you look for difficulties there, perhaps Germany will allow us this freedom.

of Copernicus himself . . . who procured immortal fame among a few but . . . [by most has been] derided and dishonored. I would dare publish my thoughts if there were many like you; but, since there are not, I shall forebear. [12]

Galileo Considers Bruno and Tycho

In the years immediately following his letter to Kepler, Galileo continued to refrain from publicly endorsing the Copernican model of the heavens. That this careful, conservative course was wise was reinforced in 1600 when the church permanently silenced one of his colleagues. The offender was Giordano Bruno, a former Dominican friar who became a scholar and outspoken supporter of Copernicus's theory. A brilliant theorist in his own right, Bruno extended the heliocentric concept to include planetary systems orbiting other stars and even intelligent beings inhabiting said planets. In 1585, in a work titled *The Ash Wednesday Supper*, he stated:

> Our world, called the terrestrial globe, is identical as far as material composition goes with the other worlds, the [orbiting] bodies of other stars; and . . . it is childish to . . . believe otherwise. Also . . . there live and strive on them [the distant planets] many and innumerable . . . individuals to no less extent than we see these living and growing on the back of this [Earth]. . . . Aristotle and others are blinded so as not to perceive the motion of the Earth to be true and necessary. They are, indeed, so inhibited that they cannot believe this [the motion of Earth] to be possible. But once this is admitted, many secrets of nature, hitherto hidden, do unfold. [13]

As Galileo was painfully aware, Bruno paid a terrible price for openly advocating such ideas. Always on the run from Catholic authorities in Rome, Bruno traveled throughout Europe. In 1591 he made the mistake of returning to Italy, where a nobleman whom he thought was his friend denounced him to the Inquisition. The Inquisition jailed Bruno. And when he refused to give up his beliefs about the universe, he was convicted of heresy (denying or opposing the truth of church doctrine) and burned at the stake in Rome in February 1600.

An Intellectual Rebel

Giordano Bruno, who, like Galileo, had a run-in with the church over the heliocentric theory, was born in Nola, Italy, in 1548. Bruno studied for the priesthood in Naples. But in 1576, shortly after being ordained a Dominican priest, he changed his mind, gave up his priestly duties, and began to travel around Europe. He became an intellectual rebel and ardent supporter of the heliocentric theory of the heavens as outlined by Nicolaus Copernicus. In 1584, in London, he published two works that advocated this view: *The Ash Wednesday Supper* and *On the Infinite Universe and Worlds*. As long as he stayed in Protestant countries, the Catholic Inquisition could not touch Bruno. But in 1591 he made the mistake of visiting Venice, where a supposed friend turned him in. Bruno was imprisoned and then tried as a heretic in Rome. Till the end, he refused to recant his views, and in 1600 the Inquisition ordered that he be burned at the stake.

Giordano Bruno was executed in 1600 for advocating the heliocentric theory.

This incident showed that it was clearly not yet safe to advocate Copernican views openly. But the church *was* willing to consider views that contradicted Aristotle, provided that they did not contradict the Scriptures as well. This was the approach used by another of Galileo's scientific colleagues, Danish astronomer Tycho Brahe. Tycho (as he was commonly called) flatly rejected Aristotle's idea of heavenly spheres, but felt that sufficient proof was still lacking for Copernicus's heliocentric system. This inspired the ingenious Dane to invent a new system of his own. In it, the other planets revolved around the Sun, but the Sun, carrying them along, itself revolved around an unmoving Earth. Because it was a geocentric conception of the universe—one in which Earth occupied the center—the church had no problem with it. But Galileo did. And his refusal to accept Tycho's version eventually played a role in Galileo's confrontation with the Inquisition. Its members could understand why he rejected some of Aristotle's ideas. But they were perplexed that he would reject Tycho's system, which seemed to them a perfectly logical alternative that did not question the truth of the Scriptures.

Telescopic Evidence

Galileo believed that the church's stance on the structure of the heavens was based on faulty reasoning because it elevated the value of tradition above that of scientific proof. In his view, there was no more convincing evidence for Tycho's system than there was for Aristotle's. Granted, proof for Copernicus's views was not yet overwhelming either. So as the years went by, Galileo searched for solid, unquestionable evidence to support the heliocentric theory.

One of several telescopes Galileo built in the early 1600s. He first used the instrument to study celestial bodies late in 1609.

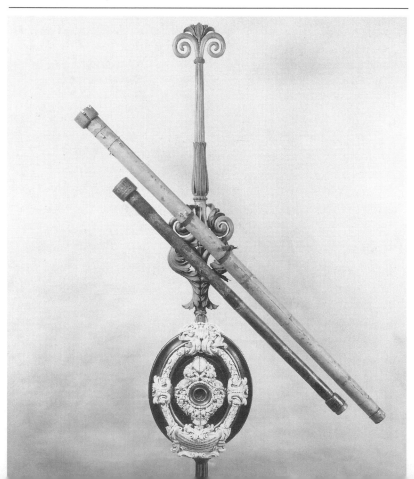

Galileo finally provided that evidence thanks to a new revolutionary invention—the telescope. In the summer of 1609, he heard that some Dutch spectacle makers had created a device that used a system of lenses to magnify distant objects three or four times. Galileo felt confident that he could build an even more powerful telescope. After experimenting with lenses, he produced an instrument that magnified nine times; soon afterward, he built one with a magnification of twenty times. In November 1609, he pointed this device at the Moon and was surprised to see its surface covered with rough features, including craters and mountain chains.

Even more startling was a discovery Galileo made on January 7, 1610. In observing the planet Jupiter, he spied three tiny starlike dots near the planet. Further observations over the next few nights revealed that the dots were moving and then a fourth dot appeared, which had apparently been hidden behind the planet's disk. Galileo became convinced that these objects were moons circling Jupiter in the manner that the Moon orbits Earth. In his mind, this was compelling evidence for the Copernican theory, or at least it demonstrated that the geocentric view was false. "Up to this time," MacLachlan explains,

> Aristotelians had argued that the Earth was the center of the universe because everything seemed to revolve around it, and no other object was the center of any rotations. Now, with moons in orbit around Jupiter, that argument was clearly invalid. [14]

Galileo wasted no time in announcing his recent telescopic discoveries. In March 1610 he published a sixty-page booklet, the *Starry Messenger*, written in Latin so that scholars all over Europe could read it. (Latin was the universal language of both scholarship and the Catholic Church.) The work quickly sold out and made Galileo famous. He sent a copy, along with a telescope, to Cosimo II, Grand Duke of Tuscany, who appointed the scientist to the position of first mathematician of his court. Galileo also resigned from the University of Padua and gained the post of chief mathematician at the University of Pisa.

Although Galileo was pleased by his fame and new prestigious positions, he was dismayed that most scholars did not appreciate

GALILEO'S FAMILY

In the same period (circa 1600) in which Giordano Bruno was executed by the church, Galileo began raising a family. While in Padua, Galileo met and began living with a young woman named Marina Gamba. They never married. But they did have three children together—Virginia, Livia, and Vincenzio (named after the scientist's father). A few years later, Marina married another man, leaving Galileo with the burden of caring for the two girls. (Vincenzio stayed with his mother.) Believing it was in their best interests, in 1613 the scientist arranged to have Virginia and Livia committed to a convent located south of Florence. Virginia, who became known as Sister Maria Celeste, thereafter corresponded regularly by letter with her father until December 1633.

---

the importance of his discoveries. Some claimed that when they looked through a telescope they could not see the moons of Jupiter; others saw the moons but held that these objects could easily be explained and accounted for by Tycho's conception of the heavens. Still others declined even to look into the telescope. About the latter, Galileo wrote to Kepler: "What would you say of the learned [men] here [in Italy] who . . . have steadfastly refused to cast a glance through the telescope? What shall we make of all this? Shall we laugh or shall we cry?" [15]

Taking a Dangerous Path

After the publication of the *Starry Messenger*, Galileo continued to make telescopic discoveries. These included the phases of the planet Venus (which showed that Venus moved around the Sun, not Earth) and the existence of dark spots on the Sun. Some scholars proposed that the sunspots were not actually on the Sun's surface but were instead small stars moving between Earth and the Sun. But Galileo concluded that these spots were indeed discolorations of the Sun itself. Observing them over time, he was able to show that the Sun rotates on its axis in about a month. In March 1613, he published his *Letters on Sunspots*, which summarized his findings.

Letters on Sunspots was important because in it Galileo publicly advocated the Copernican system for the first time. This naturally stirred up controversy, since the Scriptures feature several passages that seem to suggest that the Sun moves through the sky and Earth rests motionless. Most often cited to refute Copernicus was a tract from the Book of Joshua. This passage states that when the Hebrews were attacking some enemies, God commanded the Sun to stand still. Why would God halt the Sun, asked those who opposed the Copernican system, if it was not moving in the first place? This was a difficult question to answer unless one was audacious enough to suggest that the Scriptures should not always be taken so literally. Galileo had entered onto a dangerous path, one that had put him on a collision course with two thousand years of cherished religious tradition.

Chapter 2

The New Astronomy vs. the Holy Scriptures

IN 1610 GALILEO had been surprised and disappointed when some high-placed individuals, both inside and outside of the church, had refused to peer through his telescopes. He had sincerely hoped that the direct visual evidence afforded by the new invention would be a huge boost for the Copernican theory. He had expected that many learned people would be fascinated and open-minded enough at least to consider and debate the theory. And he had hoped that the human thirst for knowledge and truth would outweigh ancient prejudice and lead to honest attempts to reconcile the Scriptures with the new astronomy. But when many educated people responded in a lukewarm manner to the telescopic evidence, Galileo realized that he had been overly optimistic.

This realization was reinforced three years later by a number of negative reactions to the publication of the *Letters on Sunspots,* which endorsed the Copernican system. To be sure, some prominent churchmen praised the work. Galileo's friend Cardinal Maffeo Barberini, a top Vatican official, for example, wrote to the scientist to congratulate him. However, most clergymen were far less enthusiastic. Although Galileo's critics did not speak out against him in public right away, they assailed him and the Copernican theory in private gatherings, most often invoking passages from the Bible to support their position. One was the excerpt from Joshua in which God had made the Sun stand still. Further biblical proof cited to show that the Sun moved around Earth came from Ecclesiastes, which states that "the Sun rises and the Sun goes down.

Then it presses on to the place where it rises." [16] To show that Earth did not move, as Copernicus had claimed, the critics cited Psalms, which says: "The Lord . . . has made the world firm, not to be moved." [17]

Galileo was well aware of these scriptural passages that seemed to refute the heliocentric view. And it did not surprise him that some of the more conservative Catholics, clergymen and laypersons alike, would fall back on them. What disturbed him was that the number of his critics, as well as the intensity of their defense of the Scriptures, seemed to be growing. Galileo eventually decided that it would be prudent to try to meet this challenge head-on. In another burst of overblown optimism, he came to believe that he could reason with his opponents in a friendly manner and show

This seventeenth-century painting depicts Pope Paul V granting the office of cardinal to Maffeo Barberini, who praised Galileo's work.

them how the new astronomy and the Scriptures might coexist together in harmony. At the time, he could scarcely imagine the enormity of the mistake he was making. The reality was that the unfortunate series of events that would eventually lead to his humiliating trial had begun.

The Letter to Castelli

In December 1613, Galileo came upon what he thought was an opportune occasion to counter the scriptural arguments that had been leveled against him and the Copernican theory. His former student, Benedetto Castelli, now a Benedictine monk and a mathematician at the University of Pisa, had recently written to him to describe an incident that had occurred at a dinner party at the court of Grand Duke Cosimo II. According to Castelli, the guests had engaged in a major discussion about Galileo's telescopic discoveries, and Cosimo's mother, the Grand Duchess Christina, had expressed concern that Galileo's interpretation of these discoveries seemed to contradict the Scriptures.

Galileo responded in a long, carefully worded letter to Castelli. This was a calculated move intended to convey his views to both his supporters and his opponents. In a society without daily newspapers, radio, television, and other mass media, both knowledge of current events and long-range discussions of ideas depended in large degree on letter writing. Galileo knew full well that it was common practice in educated circles for important or controversial letters to be copied and passed on to others. And he expected Castelli to circulate the letter to the appropriate people.

The main goal of the letter was to effect a compromise between the new astronomy and the Scriptures that would hopefully maintain the integrity and truth of both. Indeed, Galileo was still a devout Christian who revered and respected the Bible. He simply felt that people should be careful not to take the words in the Scriptures too literally; in his view, as well as that of Castelli and several other churchmen, to do so neither flattered God nor clarified God's true lessons for humanity.

For example, as Galileo pointed out in the letter, many biblical passages describe God in physical and emotional terms that are

COS·MED·MAG·ÆTRVRI PRINCEPS·FERD·F·

Grand Duke Cosimo II as a young man. The duke's mother, Grand Duchess Christina, expressed concern that Galileo's work might contradict the Scriptures.

so human that they demean the deity. To believe such things, he said, "It would be necessary to attribute to God feet, hands and eyes, as well as bodily and human feelings like anger, regret, hate and sometimes even forgetfulness of things past and ignorance of future ones." These descriptions, he continued, were meant to "accommodate the incapacity of common people," that is, to make difficult religious concepts more easily understandable to people with little or no education (who made up the bulk of the population). Thus, "in order to adapt itself to the understanding of all people, it was appropriate for the Scriptures to say many things which are different from absolute truth, in appearance and in regard to the meaning of the words." [18] The real truths of the natural world, Galileo wrote, likely lie hidden between the lines, so to speak, of the scriptural texts.

Given that many truths are thus hidden in the Bible, Galileo continued, they are not always easy to discern and interpret. The wise person seeking to interpret the Scriptures, he wrote, must "strive to find the true meanings of scriptural passages agreeing with those physical conclusions of which we are already certain and sure from clear sensory experience or from necessary demon-

THE SCRIPTURES SIMPLIFIED FOR THE MASSES?

In this section of his famous letter to former student Benedetto Castelli (quoted in volume 5 of *Le Opere di Galileo Galilei*), Galileo argues that the wording of the Bible is sometimes simplified or colored in order to make it understandable to the uneducated masses.

The Scripture cannot err, nevertheless some of its interpreters . . . can sometimes err in various ways. One of these would be very serious and very frequent, namely to want to limit oneself always to the literal meaning of the words; for there would thus emerge not only various contradictions but also serious heresies and blasphemies, and it would be necessary to attribute to God feet, hands and eyes, as well as bodily and human feelings like anger, regret, hate and sometimes even forgetfulness of things past and ignorance of future ones. Thus in the Scripture one finds many propositions which look different from the truth if one goes by the literal meaning of the words, but which are expressed in this manner to accommodate the incapacity of common people. . . . In order to adapt itself to the understanding of all people, it was appropriate for the Scripture to say many things which are different from absolute truth, in appearance and in regard to the meaning of the words. . . . Indeed, because of the aim of adapting itself to the capacity of unrefined and undisciplined peoples, the Scripture has not abstained from somewhat concealing its most basic dogmas, thus attributing to God himself properties contrary to and very far from his essence.

strations." Furthermore, it would not be wise to force people to adhere to literal readings of the Scriptures, since this would only impede the growth of knowledge and scientific progress. "Who wants to fix a limit for the human mind?" Galileo asked Castelli in the letter. "Who wants to assert that everything which is knowable in the world is already known?" [19]

The Attacks Begin

It took several months for copies of the letter to Castelli to circulate through the noble and intellectual circles of northern Italy. As this was happening, Galileo began to realize that the letter might actually have the opposite effect of the one he had intended. "The battle was not yet completely in the open," as Jerome Langford puts it. "But the lines were being drawn up. Theologians and laypeople were taking sides." [20]

The first strong broadside against Galileo and the Copernican system came in December 1614. A prominent Dominican monk, Tommaso Caccini, preached a fiery sermon in one of Florence's major churches. Mathematics (and by inference, science in general) was the work of the devil, Caccini said, and mathematicians should be driven out of Christian communities. Caccini also argued that recent claims that Earth moves around the Sun were dangerous heresy or close to it. A few days later, a concerned Castelli wrote to Galileo:

> I am most displeased that the ignorance of some people has peaked so that, condemning sciences of which they are totally ignorant, they attribute false things to sciences they are incapable of understanding. . . . But [you must learn to have] patience; for these [insulting attacks] are neither the first nor the last. [21]

Castelli was right in his prediction that the attacks would continue. About a month after Caccini's public denunciation of the heliocentric theory, a Dominican friar and teacher named Niccolo Lorini got his hands on a copy of Galileo's letter to Castelli. Lorini did not pretend to be an expert on astronomy and knew practically nothing about Copernicus and his revolutionary views. But the priest vehemently objected to the idea of a layperson like Galileo having the gall to lecture theologians on how to interpret the Scriptures. Worried that this would encourage other nonchurchmen to question the truth of holy writ, Lorini sent a copy of the controversial letter to Cardinal Paolo Sfrondrato, one of the leaders of the Inquisition. Lorini included a note that read in part:

> [Galileo's] letter [to Castelli] contains many statements which seem presumptuous or suspect, as when it states that the words of Holy Scripture do not mean what they say; that in discussions of natural phenomena, the authority of Scripture should rank last. . . . When I saw that . . . the followers of Galileo . . . tried to defend an opinion which seemed quite contrary to the sacred text . . . I decided to acquaint Your Lordship with the state of affairs that you, in your pious zeal for the faith, may . . . provide such remedies as may appear advisable. [22]

On the surface, Lorini's letter seemed to be little more than a standard complaint and contained no overt or vicious attacks on Galileo. But some compelling evidence suggests that Lorini wanted to destroy Galileo and anyone who had the audacity to question the literal wording of the Scriptures. Unbeknownst to the inquisitor Sfrondrato, in copying Galileo's letter to Castelli, Lorini made a number of alterations that distorted Galileo's original meaning and made it appear that the scientist was denying the truth of the Scriptures. For example, Galileo had written, "There are in Scripture words which, when taken in the strict literal meaning, look as if they differed from the truth." Lorini changed the sentence to "There are in Scripture words which are false in their literal meaning." [23]

Bellarmine's Note of Caution

Luckily for Galileo, he was able, at least in the short term, to forestall any major damage to his reputation. He sent an unaltered copy of the letter to a friend in Rome, who conveyed it to Cardinal Robert Bellarmine, a leading theologian and a member of the Inquisition. After examining both versions of the letter, the

Galileo explained his views to his friend Castelli in a letter that aroused the censure of several prominent church officials.

Catholic inquisitors found nothing that they felt constituted heresy. The much relieved Galileo was encouraged by this and also by an incident that soon followed. In March 1615, a priest from Naples, Paolo Foscarini, published a pamphlet that argued that the Copernican theory did not contradict the Scriptures. The fact that a leading clergyman had come out in support of Copernicus made Galileo feel hopeful that it was now becoming acceptable to have serious discussions about the heliocentric theory.

A note of caution, however, soon appeared. Foscarini sent a copy of his pamphlet to Cardinal Bellarmine. Bellarmine quickly responded to Foscarini, and made sure to send a copy of the letter, dated April 12, 1615, to Galileo, whom he knew held ideas similar to those of Foscarini. "It seems to me," Bellarmine began,

> that your Reverence and Signor Galileo act prudently when you content yourselves with speaking hypothetically and not absolutely, as I have always understood that Copernicus spoke. . . . But to want to affirm that the Sun, in very truth, is at the center of the universe and only rotates on its axis without going from east to west, is a very dangerous attitude and one calculated . . . to injure our holy faith by contradicting the Scriptures. . . . As you are aware, the Council of Trent [a series of church reforms enacted between 1543 and 1565] forbids the interpretation of the Scriptures in a way contrary to the common opinion of the holy Fathers. . . . The Sun is in the heavens and revolves round the Earth with immense speed and the Earth is very distant from the heavens, at the center of the universe, and motionless. Consider, then, in your prudence, whether the church can tolerate that the Scriptures should be interpreted in a manner contrary to that of the holy Fathers. . . . If there were a real proof that the Sun is in the center of the universe . . . and

THE WISDOM OF SOLOMON

In this excerpt from his letter to Father Foscarini (quoted in volume 12 of *Le Opere di Galileo Galilei*), Cardinal Bellarmine claims that the heliocentric theory cannot be true, since the great and infallible ancient Israelite king, Solomon, stated clearly that the Sun moves.

> The idea that the Sun stands still and the Earth moves around it must . . . be an illusion. The man who wrote: The Earth abideth forever; the Sun also riseth, and the Sun goeth down, and hasteth to his place whence he arose, was Solomon, who not only spoke by divine inspiration but was wise and learned, above all others, in human sciences and in the knowledge of created things. As he had all this wisdom from God Himself, it is not likely that he would have made a statement contrary to a truth, either proven or capable of proof.

that the Sun does not go round the Earth . . . then we should
have [great difficulty] in explaining passages of Scripture
which appear to teach the contrary. . . . In case of doubt we
ought not to abandon the interpretation of the sacred text
as given by the holy Fathers. [24]

Two essential points emerged from Bellarmine's letter. First,
it was acceptable to discuss Copernicus's ideas about Earth, the
Sun, and the universe, as long as they were understood to be mere
hypotheses, that is, unproved propositions. To say that they were
demonstrated fact would contradict Holy Scripture, which was a
dangerous course to take. Second, Bellarmine made it clear that
the version of the universe given in the Scriptures must remain
the accepted one until definitive proof emerged to show it was
wrong.

The Church Bans Copernicus

Galileo appreciated Bellarmine's position. But he worried that the
church was being too inflexible and that refusing to accept the
Copernican system would ultimately hurt its reputation and authority. Against the advice of friends, the impatient and often impul-
sive Galileo decided to go to Rome. There, he hoped to explain
his position, as well as Copernicus's ideas, to leading intellectuals
and thereby hasten its acceptance by the church.

After arriving in Rome in December 1615, Galileo attended
numerous gatherings at private homes and impressed his fellow
guests with both his great knowledge and his boldness in championing controversial scientific ideas. Antonio Querengo, a nobleman who witnessed Galileo in some of these sessions, later penned
this illuminating description:

We have here Mr. Galileo, who frequently in meetings of
men with curiosity, attracts the attention of many with
regard to the opinion of Copernicus which he holds to be
true. . . . He talks frequently with fifteen or twenty guests
who argue with him now in one house, now in another. But
he is so well fortified that . . . he shows up as worthless the
majority of the arguments with which his opponents try to

To Galileo's regret, the church banned the heliocentric theory and Copernicus's (pictured) famous book in March 1616.

defeat him. Monday, in particular . . . he was especially effective. What I enjoyed most was that before he would answer the arguments of his opponents, he would amplify them and strengthen them with new grounds which made them appear invincible, so that, when he proceeded to demolish them, he made his opponents look all the more ridiculous. [25]

Evidently these minor victories in private settings made Galileo too overconfident for his own good. Believing that it was his duty to convince the presiding pope, Paul V, of the truth of

A bust of Pope Paul V, who presided over the banning of the heliocentric theory. Galileo failed to convince the pope that the theory was sound.

the Copernican system, he gave a written presentation of proof to a leading cardinal to pass on to the pope. Paul was irritated by what he saw as the scientist's insolence. Accordingly, the pontiff ordered a commission of cardinals to examine the Copernican theory and judge what should be done about it. On March 5, 1616, the commission officially condemned the heliocentric theory and banned a number of works that advocated it, including those by Copernicus and Foscarini.

In the meantime, the pope instructed Cardinal Bellarmine to speak to Galileo and warn him that he must abandon his support of the Copernican theory or risk imprisonment. A document later found in church files and dated February 26, 1616, states in part:

> At the palace, the usual residence of Lord Cardinal Bellarmine, the said Galileo . . . [was] warned of the error of the [Copernican theory] and admonished to abandon it; and immediately thereafter . . . the Lord Cardinal being present, the said Galileo was . . . commanded . . . to relinquish altogether the said opinion that the Sun is the center of the world and immovable and that the Earth moves; nor further to hold, teach, or defend it in any way whatsoever, verbally or in writing; otherwise proceedings would be taken against him by the Holy Office; which injunction the said Galileo . . . promised to obey. [26]

Modern scholars believe that this account may not accurately describe what transpired at the meeting. The injunction (command) given to Galileo, which years later was to have a crucial bearing on the course of his trial, may well have been false. It appears that Galileo did meet with Bellarmine in February 1616. However, many modern scholars believe that the real record of the meeting, in which Bellarmine told Galileo he could talk about Copernicus's theory only as an unproved hypothesis, was destroyed. In its place, according to this view, an altered version was planted by Galileo's enemies, one that suggested that he

THE DECREE BANNING COPERNICUS

Following is part of the church decree of March 5, 1616, that banned Copernicus's book and others that advocated the heliocentric theory. It can be found in volume 19 of *Le Opere di Galileo Galilei*.

> In regard to several books containing various heresies and errors, to prevent the emergence of more serious harm throughout Christendom, the Holy Congregation of the Most Illustrious Lord Cardinals . . . has decided that they should be altogether condemned and prohibited. . . . It orders that henceforth no one, of whatever station or condition, should dare print them, or have them printed, or read them, or have them in one's possession in any way . . . [and] whoever is now or will be in the future in possession of them is required to surrender them to . . . inquisitors, immediately after learning of the present decree. [A list of the banned books follows]. . . . In witness thereof, this decree has been signed by the hand and stamped with the seal of the Most Illustrious and Reverend Lord Cardinal of St. Cecilia, Bishop of Albano, on 5 March 1616.

had agreed never again to "hold, teach, or defend" the Copernican theory.

The New Pope

However strict the injunction Galileo received in 1616 may have been, he was understandably upset about the banning of Copernicus's book and the harm it might do to scientific progress. He was also afraid of what might happen to him. So during the next few years Galileo was careful not to advocate the truth of the heliocentric theory in public. The situation seemed to change for the better, however, when in 1623 Galileo's old friend and supporter Cardinal Maffeo Barberini became Pope Urban VIII. Galileo felt as though fortune had suddenly smiled on him. Earlier, when still a cardinal, Barberini had often expressed his admiration for the scientist. Once when Galileo was ill, the cardinal had written:

> I write because men like you, who are of great value, deserve to live a long time for the public benefit, and I am

also motivated by the particular interest and affection which I have for you, and by my constant approbation [praise] of you and your work. [27]

Galileo visited Rome again in the spring of 1624 and was well received by the pope, who met with the scientist six times. Urban told Galileo that he could write about Copernicus's ideas if he did not claim that they were the only true explanations for the workings of the universe. Copernicus's book was banned only because it made such a claim, Urban said. The basic ideas in the book were not prohibited as long as they were labeled unsupported theories. The pope claimed that he had no objections to people discussing various unproven hypotheses about astronomy, including those of Copernicus. Indeed, in his mind "unproven" was the operative word. "As far as he was concerned," Langford writes,

a strict [definitive and unarguable] demonstration of any system of the universe was impossible. . . . His reasoning was that God, who is all powerful, could have established the machinery of the universe in such a way that no man could ever penetrate its mysteries. Thus, even if all the evidence seemed to prove one system in preference to another, it could not be said to be demonstrated because true demonstration demands full certitude [assurance] that the conclusion is true and cannot be otherwise. As far as Urban was concerned, this kind of certitude could exist only in the mind of God. [28]

Thus, the pope seemed to be saying that as long as a nontraditional theory of the universe was not promoted as the only true one, it was safe to talk about that theory. Urban's words helped to rekindle a spirit of hope in Galileo. Also encouraging was the way the scientist continued to be welcomed in high religious circles in Rome in the years that followed. The pope, his secretary Giovanni Ciampoli, and many other leading churchmen greatly admired Galileo and enjoyed reading his works. And they continued to urge him to write more. Of even greater importance, the evidence shows that they led him to believe that he could advance any theory as long as he prefaced it with a disclaimer stating that it was not the final word on the subject.

In the mid-1620s, in an optimistic mind-set, Galileo began work on a major volume about astronomy. It would, he hoped, once and for all convince educated people that Copernicus had been right. In the long run, the book did turn out to be instrumental in accomplishing that goal. But this was not destined to happen in Galileo's own lifetime. For him, the *Dialogue Concerning the Two Chief World Systems,* one of the greatest works of early modern science, would prove a major element in his ultimate undoing.

Chapter 3

Galileo on Trial: The Initial Depositions

E NCOURAGED BY THE friendly attitude of Pope Urban and other leading churchmen, Galileo worked on his new book throughout the late 1620s. Finally, in December 1629, the initial draft of the *Dialogue Concerning the Two Chief World Systems*, usually referred to more simply as the *Dialogue*, was completed. It was reviewed by the official Catholic censor in Rome, who asked for some changes, and Galileo made the changes. The volume was published in February 1632 and quickly sold out. Yet only a few months later, the Catholic Church reversed itself, suspended further publication of the book, and ordered the author to stand trial on suspicion of heresy.

A Simpleton vs. the Voice of Reason

To understand why the church so suddenly changed its position and transformed Galileo's proudest moment into his darkest one, one must first consider the particulars of the *Dialogue* itself. Galileo called it a dialogue because it consists of a fictional conversation among three men. The main character, named Salviati, was based on a deceased friend of Galileo's from Florence and is the spokesman for the author's own ideas. The second character, Sagredo, was named after another of Galileo's dead friends. Lastly comes the character Simplicio, a defender of Aristotle's views who, as his name suggests, is a simpleminded individual.

The conversation these three men have takes place over the course of four days. So the book has four sections: Day One, Day

Two, Day Three, and Day Four. Arguments about the movements of Earth and the Sun occur primarily in Days Three and Four, with Simplicio defending the traditional geocentric view against Salviati, who advocates the heliocentric theory. In Day Three, for example, Simplicio says: "The Earth is at the center [of the heavens],

A seventeenth-century artist's rendition of the three characters that argue in Galileo's Dialogue Concerning the Two Chief World Systems.

as is proved in many ways by Aristotle, Ptolemy, and others."
Salviati replies:

> It is quite certain that not the Earth, but the Sun, is to be
> found at the center of the universe. Hence, as for this first
> general conception, the central place is the Sun's, and the
> Earth is to be found as far away from the center as it is from
> the Sun. . . . This is deduced from most obvious and there-
> fore most powerfully convincing observations. The most
> palpable of these, which excludes the Earth from the cen-
> ter and places the Sun here, is that we find all the planets
> closer to the Earth at one time and farther from it at another.
> The differences are so great that Venus, for example, is six
> times as distant from us at its farthest as at its closest, and
> Mars soars nearly eight times as high in the one state as in
> the other. You may thus see whether Aristotle was not some
> trifle deceived in believing that they were always equally
> distant from us.[29]

This excerpt from the book highlights the main problem that a
number of leading churchmen and inquisitors had with it after it
was published. Salviati has by far the longest, most detailed speeches.

SIMPLICIO'S DISCLAIMER

In this excerpt from the last section of his *Dialogue Concerning the
Two Chief World Systems* (Stillman Drake's translation), Galileo supplied
the disclaimer that he mistakenly thought would satisfy the church.
It is voiced by the slow-witted character Simplicio.

> As to the discourses we have held [about the notion that Earth
> moves, and especially that said movement causes the tides] . . .
> I am really not entirely convinced. . . . I do not therefore con-
> sider them true and conclusive. Indeed . . . I know that, if asked
> whether God in His infinite power and wisdom could have
> [caused the motions of the tides] using some other means, both
> of you would reply that He could have, and that He would have
> known how to do this in many ways which are unthinkable to
> our minds. From this I . . . conclude that . . . it would be exces-
> sive boldness for anyone to limit and restrict the Divine power
> and wisdom to some particular fancy of his own [such as the
> heliocentric view].

Furthermore, he and his clearly Copernican-Galilean views are always portrayed as the voice of reason, while the counterarguments given by Simplicio are mostly short, muddled, and generally unconvincing. The volume is a thinly veiled argument for the Copernican theory, and the church eventually recognized it as such.

Although the chief censor, Niccolo Riccardi, approved publication of the *Dialogue,* he did so quite reluctantly. Riccardi personally liked and often supported Galileo, but he was convinced the work was pro-Copernican and would cause trouble for both Galileo and the church. On the one hand, the censor knew that Urban had encouraged the scientist to write it; on the other, the pope's secretary, Ciampoli, and others who liked Galileo heavily pressured Riccardi to approve the volume. Riccardi finally gave in, against his better judgment. And sure enough, after publication most of the conservative churchmen began denouncing the book, just as he had worried they would.

The other problem was that Pope Urban abruptly turned on Galileo and joined the chorus of critics. This was primarily because of the author's own poor judgment. The obligatory "submission clause"—the statement that the ideas discussed were only hypotheses and that humans could never hope to understand God's true secrets—was extremely brief. It also came at the very end of the book, almost as an afterthought. Even worse, Galileo placed these all-important words in the mouth of the dim-witted Simplicio. After the book was published, some of Galileo's enemies at the Vatican convinced Urban that he himself was the model for Simplicio and that the scientist was mocking him. Offended and feeling betrayed, Urban angrily ordered that sales of the *Dialogue* be halted and turned the matter over to the Inquisition.

Galileo Ordered to Stand Trial

The die was now cast for Galileo. Late in 1632, he received orders from the Inquisition to appear in Rome to stand trial on suspicion of heresy. At first, illness delayed him. But then the pope sent word that if he did not come at once he would be arrested and dragged in chains. Galileo, now almost sixty-nine and still sick, arrived in Rome in February 1633. He stayed there in comfortable quarters in the Tuscan embassy for the next two months. (Because they were still separate nations at the time, Tuscany, Venice, and other Italian states had foreign embassies in Rome, capital of the Papal States.)

In early April, Galileo was finally transferred to the building that housed the offices of the Inquisition. He was told that he would be confined there during the course of the trial. But he was not thrown into a dungeon, as was sometimes erroneously reported in later descriptions of his trial. In fact, out of respect for his fame and friendship with many high church leaders, he was given a comfortable suite of rooms and was assigned a servant to help him with his daily needs.

The trial began on April 12, 1633. It was not a formal public proceeding like those familiar today, with lawyers representing and arguing for each side, a judge keeping order, and an impartial jury listening to the evidence. Instead, what the church then called a trial consisted of a series of private proceedings that are better described as informal hearings. On four separate occasions, two inquisitors questioned or took statements from Galileo while a secretary kept notes of what was said.

In each questioning, called a deposition, the inquisitors tried to establish for the record what was already a foregone conclusion in their minds. Namely, the scientist was guilty of heresy for openly advocating, defending, and teaching the Copernican system, which had been prohibited by the church in 1616. Thus, the questioners were somewhat equivalent to the prosecutors in a modern trial. During these depositions, Galileo was allowed to make statements in his own defense. (Later, the inquisitors reported the outcomes of the depositions to ten cardinals who had been selected to be Galileo's judges. In what constituted the second part of the trial, the cardinals debated what sentence to give the scientist and imposed that sentence, based mostly on the notes of the depositions and the recommendations of a small group of churchmen who closely examined the *Dialogue*.)

The First Deposition

It is unknown whether Galileo stood or sat while facing his questioners. What is more certain are the questions and answers, which have survived. As the first deposition began, the court asked Galileo when he had arrived in Rome and why he had come. He answered:

POPE URBAN VIII

This informative brief biography of Galileo's friend-turned-enemy, Pope Urban VIII (born Maffeo Barberini), is by scholar Douglas Linder (from his online collection of materials about Galileo and the church).

Maffeo Barberini was born into a powerful family of Florentine merchants. . . . [He] earned a doctor of law degree from the University of Pisa, [then] rose rapidly in the church hierarchy. In 1606, he was appointed cardinal and, with the death of Pope Gregory XV in 1623, he was elected Pope, taking the name of Pope Urban VIII. As Pope, Urban VIII made it his goal to reinvigorate papal power [which had been waning in recent years]. In the early days of his reign, Galileo had reason to believe Maffeo Barberini's elevation to Pope might lead to a loosening of the church's opposition to Copernican thought. Pope Urban VIII received Galileo for six long audiences. . . . [The Pope] seemed genuinely interested in Galileo's ideas . . . [and] assured Galileo that as long as he

Pope Urban VIII initially supported Galileo, but later opposed him.

remained Pope, the memory of Copernicus had nothing to fear. Eventually, however, the Pope's pride and suspicions would produce the dramatic confrontation with Galileo that culminated with his arrest, trial, and conviction in 1633.

I arrived in Rome the first Sunday of Lent. . . . In Florence the Father Inquisitor ordered me to come to Rome and present myself to the Holy Office, this being an injunction by the officials of the Holy Office. I imagine that the reason why I have been ordered to present myself to the Holy Office in Rome is to account for my recently printed book. . . . It is a book written in dialogue form, and it treats of the constitution of the world, that is, of the two chief systems, and the arrangement of the heavens and the elements.[30]

The inquisitors then asked Galileo to name the book and identify it as his. And he did so.

Having dispensed with the preliminaries, the court got down to the nitty-gritty of its case against Galileo. For the Inquisition, the question of whether the *Dialogue* did or did not openly advocate the Copernican view was secondary. The questioners concentrated instead on getting Galileo to admit that back in 1616, when called before Cardinal Bellarmine, he had promised not to advocate or teach Copernicus's ideas as natural truths. Since Copernicus was already banned by the church, all that was needed to convict the scientist was evidence that he had broken his promise and openly defended and taught the heliocentric theory as fact.

In response to this accusation, Galileo insisted that he could not remember making such a promise to Cardinal Bellarmine. And

This depiction of Galileo confronting the Inquisition exaggerates the number of inquisitors present. In reality, only two men questioned him.

indeed, this may have been the truth. It now appears probable that the so-called promise may have been manufactured in 1633 by some of the conservative inquisitors who considered Galileo a threat to the church's integrity. Fortunately for Galileo, he had retained a certificate given to him by Bellarmine at the conclusion of their 1616 meeting. The note indicated only that the cardinal had warned the scientist that the church now forbade people to hold or defend the Copernican theory as fact; it said nothing about a promise not to teach the theory. With the certificate in hand, Galileo told the inquisitors:

> The occasion for my being in Rome in the year 1616 was that, having heard objections to Nicolas Copernicus's opinion on the Earth's motion, the Sun's stability, and the arrangement of the heavenly spheres, in order to be sure of holding only holy and Catholic opinions, I came to hear what was proper to hold in regard to this topic. . . . I discussed this matter with some cardinals who oversaw the Holy Office at that time, especially with Cardinal Bellarmine. . . . [He] told me that Copernicus's opinion could be held suppositionally [i.e., as a mere hypothesis or unproved theory], as Copernicus himself had held it. His Eminence knew that I held it suppositionally, namely in the way that Copernicus held it. . . . In conformity with this I keep a certificate by Lord Cardinal Bellarmine himself, dated 26 May 1616, in which he says that Copernicus's opinion cannot be held or defended, being against Holy Scripture. I present a copy of this certificate, and here it is. . . . Finally, it may be that I was given an injunction [order] not to hold or defend the said opinion, but I do not recall it since this is something of many years ago.[31]

The inquisitors told Galileo that claiming that he did not remember Bellarmine's order was not a sufficient defense. Such a command coming from the Vatican was so important that no person could possibly forget it, no matter how many years had since gone by. But Galileo strenuously insisted that he could not recollect any such order. "I do not recall that I was told anything else," he said,

> nor can I know whether I shall remember what was then told me, even if it is read to me. I am saying freely what I recall because I do not claim not to have in any way violated that injunction, that is, not to have held or defended at all the said opinion of the Earth's motion and Sun's stability. I do not recall that this injunction was given me. . . . Regarding the . . . phrases in the said injunction now mentioned, namely not to teach [the Copernican theory] and in any way whatever, I did not retain them in my memory, I think because they are not contained in the said certificate, which I relied upon and kept as a reminder. [32]

Urging Galileo to Confess

As the first deposition ended, the inquisitors found themselves in an unexpected bind. They had their own record of the 1616 meeting, which, forged or not, was the cornerstone of their case. Yet out of nowhere, Galileo had revealed the existence of Bellarmine's certificate, which gave a contradictory account. Moreover, they could not deny that the note was authentic.

Still, the Inquisition was confident that it could easily prove the scientist's guilt. Both during and after the first deposition, three special religious counselors appointed by the Inquisition examined the *Dialogue*. They concluded that it did indeed advocate the Copernican system as the one true system and that it mocked those who disagreed with Copernicus as mental inferiors. This alone seemed to be enough to convict Galileo.

Meanwhile, however, several high-placed men in the Inquisition were working behind the scenes to help Galileo. They agreed that he was probably guilty of advocating the heliocentric view. But they felt that he was a brilliant and good man and that more conservative and mean-spirited elements within the Inquisition were trying too hard to humiliate him. On April 27, the sympathetic Father Vincenzio Firenzuola met privately with Galileo and

This first edition of Galileo's Dialogue *is housed in a Florence museum. When first published in 1632, the book troubled many churchmen.*

tried to get him to admit his guilt. If he did so, Firenzuola was sure that it could be arranged for the scientist to get off lightly, perhaps with only a few months of house arrest. "I entered into discourse with Galileo yesterday afternoon," Firenzuola wrote on April 28,

> and after many arguments and rejoinders had passed
> between us, by God's grace, I attained my object, for I
> brought him to a full sense of his error, so that he clearly

recognized that he had erred and had gone too far in his book. And to all this he gave expression in words of much feeling, like one who experienced great consolation in the recognition of his error, and he was also willing to confess it judicially [in court]. He requested, however, a little time in order to consider the form in which he might most fittingly make the confession, which as far as its substance is concerned, will, I hope, follow in the manner indicated.[33]

The Second Deposition

The "little time" Galileo requested to prepare his confession turned out to be three days, as the second deposition took place on April 30,

Galileo (at right) waits for the start of his second deposition, during which he offered to write a new section of the Dialogue *refuting Copernicus's ideas.*

1633. Firenzuola and the others were surprised, however, when the statement Galileo made to the inquisitors consisted of only a partial confession of guilt. He told them:

> For several days I have been thinking continuously and directly about the interrogations I underwent on the 16th of this month and in particular about the question [of] whether sixteen years ago I had been prohibited, by order of the Holy Office, from holding, defending, and teaching in any way whatever the opinion, then condemned, of the Earth's motion and Sun's stability. It dawned on me to reread my printed *Dialogue*, which over the last three years I had not even looked at.[34]

The scientist went on to say that he wanted to check to make sure that he had not written "something enabling readers or superiors to infer a defect of disobedience on my part." In fact, he said, he had now found some places in the manuscript where it appeared that he had unknowingly gone too far in his explanation of the Copernican system. "I freely confess," he told the court,

> that it appeared to me in several places to be written in such a way that a reader, not aware of my intention, would have had reason to form the opinion that the arguments for the false side, which I intended to confute, were so stated as to be capable of convincing [the reader] because of their strength. . . . In particular, two arguments, one based on sunspots and the other on the tides, are presented favorably to the reader as being strong and powerful, more than would seem proper for someone who deemed them to be inconclusive and wanted to confute them.

It had been wrong of him to make these statements sound so convincing, he told the inquisitors. But it had not been intentional. "My error then was, and I confess it, one of vain ambition, pure ignorance, and inadvertence."[35]

When Galileo had finished his statement, the inquisitors declared the session to be over. A few minutes later, however, the scientist returned and asked to be allowed to add a few more words to the record. By this time he must have become extremely fearful of the wrath of the Inquisition, for he lied to them, saying that he did not believe the Copernican system to be true. Moreover, he would gladly write a new section for the *Dialogue* in which he would refute the ideas advanced in the earlier sections. "I neither did hold nor do hold as true the condemned opinion of the Earth's motion and Sun's stability," he said. "I promise to reconsider the arguments already presented in favor of the said false and condemned opinion and to confute them in the most effective way that the blessed God will enable me." [36]

The Third Deposition

The cardinals turned down Galileo's offer to add a refutation of Copernicus's ideas to the *Dialogue*. They were more interested in the fact that he had not admitted breaking his 1616 promise to Cardinal Bellarmine. Instead, he had merely confessed to "going too far" in the writing of his book. His stubbornness frustrated them. But at least he was old and sick and would not try to flee, they reasoned. So they allowed him to leave the Inquisition building and return to the Tuscan embassy while waiting for the third deposition.

That questioning took place on May 10, 1633. In it, Galileo was allowed to present a formal defense, which took the form of a written statement he had prepared over the course of the preceding eight days. In the statement, Galileo again fell back on the certificate given to him by Bellarmine in 1616. The scientist insisted that he had not promised the cardinal to refrain from teaching the Copernican theory. In the certificate, Galileo told the inquisitors,

> one clearly sees that I was only told not to hold or defend Copernicus's doctrine of the Earth's motion and Sun's stability; but one cannot see any trace that . . . I was given any other special order. . . . Thus . . . [the phrase] "teaching" . . . struck me as very new and unheard-of. I do not think I should be mistrusted about the fact that in the course of fourteen or sixteen years I lost any memory of [the matter],

GALILEO REQUESTS MERCY

Following is the section from Galileo's defense (quoted in Douglas Linder's online collection of Galileo-related materials), presented
to the Inquisition on May 10, 1633, in which he asks his accusers to
consider his poor health and advancing age.

> Finally, I am left with asking you to consider the pitiable state
> of ill health to which I am reduced, due to ten months of con-
> stant mental distress, and the discomforts of a long and tiresome
> journey in the most awful season and at the age of seventy; I
> feel I have lost the greater part of the years which my previous
> state of health promised me. I am encouraged to do this by the
> faith I have in the clemency and kindness of heart of the Most
> Eminent Lordships, my judges; and I hope that if their sense
> of justice perceives anything lacking among so many ailments
> as adequate punishment for my crimes, they will, I beg them,
> condone it out of regard for my declining old age, which I humbly
> also ask them to consider.

especially since I had no need to give the matter any thought,
having such a valid reminder in writing. [37]

Therefore, Galileo continued, he had not knowingly and willingly disobeyed the orders given to him by Cardinal Bellarmine.
Furthermore, he was ready to make up for his errors by doing whatever the inquisitors desired him to do. Galileo also asked the cardinals to take his age and poor health into consideration in decid-
ing his fate. "Equally," he added, "I want them to consider my
honor and reputation against the slanders of those who hate me." [38]

The Wishes of an Angry Pope

At this point, the court felt that the deposition phase of the trial
was over. And despite the scientist's stubbornness about the 1616
certificate, the inquisitors were apparently ready to recommend
to the panel of ten judges a fairly lenient sentence. This would be
in keeping with the informal agreement worked out between
Galileo and Father Firenzuola on April 27.

However, the best efforts of those sympathetic to Galileo were
thwarted by those who disliked and resented him. It was custom-
ary for the Inquisition to give the pope a report of the depositions

in such a high-profile case. Unfortunately for Galileo, those who prepared the report purposely slanted it to injure him. They claimed that he had insolently told the inquisitors that some parts of the Scriptures were false, for example. This was a lie.

After reading the report, Pope Urban, who already felt betrayed by Galileo, became more furious than ever. On June 16, 1633, the pope overruled Firenzuola's deal and ordered that Galileo's book be banned outright. In addition, said the pope, Galileo must renounce the heliocentric theory publicly. "His Holiness decreed that the said Galileo is to be interrogated," the official record reads, "even with the threat of torture, and . . . he is to abjure [his belief in the prohibited Copernican theory before] an assembly of the Congregation of the Holy Office, and then is to be condemned to imprisonment." [39]

This was not Galileo's formal sentence. That would come later from the panel of cardinals. But everyone knew that it was extremely unlikely that these judges would dare to contradict the emphatic wishes of an angry pope. The scientist's fate was clearly sealed.

Chapter 4

Galileo on Trial: The Sentence and Abjuration

THE INQUISITION HAD originally intended to hold no more than three depositions in Galileo's trial. These focused on getting Galileo to admit that he had broken his promise to Cardinal Bellarmine not to teach the Copernican theory and allowed him to make statements in his own defense. The issue of whether Galileo himself believed in the heliocentric theory was not directly addressed in these initial proceedings. The inquisitors who confronted the scientist felt that it could reasonably be assumed that he did believe Earth moved, since his book seemed to advocate this idea quite strongly. Their main interest was to force Galileo to confess, give him a firm slap on the wrist, and make sure that thereafter he caused the church no more embarrassment or trouble.

The situation changed, however, after the pope directly entered the fray. The angry Urban made it clear in his pronouncement of June 16, 1633, that Galileo must be dealt with more severely than the Inquisition had first intended. The scientist must make a public abjuration, the pope insisted, a humiliating renunciation of his beliefs; he must be imprisoned for a long time; and his book must be banned completely. These were serious, possibly controversial actions for the church to take. And it was understood that, before taking them, the inquisitors and judges had to make as solid a case as possible that Galileo was guilty. Before the formal sentencing and abjuration could proceed, therefore, another deposition was needed. Its aim was to prove the scientist's "intention" in writing the *Dialogue;* that is, did he or did he not personally believe that the Copernican theory was true?

The Fourth Deposition

The fourth deposition in Galileo's trial was held on June 21, 1633. Attempting to discover the true feelings of the accused about the heliocentric view, an inquisitor asked him whether he held that the Sun, rather than Earth, is the center of the heavens, and if so, how long he had held this view. Galileo answered:

During Galileo's fourth deposition before the Inquisition, the scientist lied and said he believed the Sun moved.

> A long time ago, that is, before the [Copernican theory was prohibited] . . . I was undecided and regarded the two opinions, those of Ptolemy and Copernicus, as disputable, because either the one or the other could be true in nature. But after the above-mentioned decision, assured by the prudence of the authorities, all my uncertainty stopped, and I held, as I still hold, as very true and undoubted Ptolemy's opinion, namely the stability of the Earth and the motion of the Sun.[40]

This was a bold-faced lie, of course, for Galileo believed implicitly in the Copernican system, not the geocentric system of Aristotle and Ptolemy. But at this point, he was fearful that he might languish or rot in prison and was willing to say practically anything to escape such a fate.

The inquisitors were not deceived, however. They told Galileo that many of the statements made by the character Salviati in the *Dialogue* seemed to show that the scientist did indeed believe in the heliocentric theory. And they demanded that he confess and admit his guilt. "In regard to my writing of the *Dialogue* already published," Galileo responded,

> I did not do so because I held Copernicus's opinion to be true. Instead, deeming only to be doing a beneficial service, I explained the physical and astronomical reasons that can be advanced for one side and for the other; I tried to show that none of these, neither those in favor of this opinion or that, had the strength of a conclusive proof and that therefore to proceed with certainty one had to resort to the determination of more subtle doctrines, as one can see in many places in the *Dialogue*. So for my part I conclude that I do not hold and, after the determination of the authorities, I have not held the condemned opinion. . . . I do not hold this opinion of Copernicus, and I have not held it after being ordered by injunction to abandon it. For the rest, here I am in your hands; do as you please.[41]

At this juncture, the chief inquisitor warned that if the scientist did not tell the truth the court might need to resort to torture.

THE EMPTY THREAT OF TORTURE

As pointed out by scholar Jerome J. Langford in this excerpt from his acclaimed book about Galileo's confrontation with the church, the threat of torture used in the fourth deposition was largely an empty one.

The word "torture" cited in [some of] the document[s surrounding Galileo's trial] has given rise to another legend connected with the name of Galileo, a legend which, until recently, enjoyed wide acceptance. . . . Galileo was not tortured, nor was he shown the instruments of torture. He was verbally threatened with torture. But he knew that the threat carried no weight. It was common knowledge, and [scholars] of the period are unanimous in verifying it, that no one of Galileo's age or poor health could be subjected to physical torture. Now there can be no defense of torture, or even threats of torture. But [the threat of it] here was a mere formality and Galileo knew it.

However, this threat was a mere formality, one repeated by tradition in all such cases. The church had legal rules that forbade torturing an elderly or sick person, and everyone present, including the defendant himself, knew that no torture would be applied.

The Sentence

The pope and Inquisition had hoped to get Galileo to cooperate and provide them with a strong rationale for punishing him. He had not done so. Yet the accusers were satisfied that they had performed the necessary steps to justify the harshness of the sentence to come. Although Galileo had not admitted to believing in the heliocentric view, he had at least been given the chance to admit it; and having been granted that opportunity, he had blatantly lied. In the minds of the judges, that was enough to support their handing down a sentence as severe as they saw fit.

That sentence was imposed the next day, June 22, 1633, at a Dominican convent, Santa Maria Sopra Minerva. Located in the center of Rome, the structure had been built from the ruined materials of an ancient Roman pagan temple (dedicated to Minerva, goddess of wisdom) and had a large central hall suitable for important ceremonies. Wearing a white shirt, which symbolized remorse, Galileo stood before his judges. A priest then began reading the sentence. The first section listed some basic charges, including the scientist's crimes of believing in the false doctrine that Earth moves and teaching such ideas to his followers. This was followed by a formal statement of the church's position on the heliocentric theory:

> The proposition that the Sun is the center of the world and does not move from its place is absurd and false philosophically and formally heretical, because it is expressly

The ornately decorated exterior of the convent of Santa Maria Sopra Minerva, where Galileo's abjuration took place on June 22, 1633.

contrary to Holy Scripture. The proposition that the Earth is not the center of the world and immovable but that it moves . . . is equally absurd and false . . . and theologically considered at least erroneous in faith.[42]

Next, the text of the judges' sentence reviewed the central charge of the case—that Galileo had ignored Cardinal Bellarmine's order not to advocate or teach the Copernican theory—along with the related evidence:

It was decreed . . . on the twenty-fifth of February, 1616, that his Eminence the Lord Cardinal Bellarmine should

This painting of Galileo shows him as he probably looked during his trial. He was sixty-nine at the time and had led a busy, stress-filled life.

order you to abandon altogether the said false doctrine and, in the event of your refusal, that an injunction should be imposed upon you . . . to give up the said doctrine and not to teach it to others, not to defend it, nor even to discuss it. . . . In execution of this decree, on the following day at the palace of and in the presence of the Cardinal Bellarmine . . . you were given an injunction . . . to the effect that you must completely abandon the said false opinion, and that in the future you could neither hold, nor defend, nor teach it in any way whatever, either orally or in writing; having promised to obey, you were dismissed. [43]

The next section of the judges' sentence was a reminder that the church had prohibited the reading or teaching of Copernican doctrine because it was "false and wholly contrary to the divine and Holy Scripture." Yet despite this ban, Galileo had proceeded to write his *Dialogue Concerning the Two Chief World Systems*, which the church "diligently examined and found to violate explicitly the above-mentioned injunction given to you; for in the same book you have defended the said opinion already condemned." Galileo had been examined under oath and acknowledged that the book in question was his. He had admitted that he had asked for permission to publish it without telling the censor about the promise he had given Bellarmine not to hold, defend, or teach the doctrines contained in it. Likewise, "you confessed that in several places the exposition of the said book is expressed in such a way that a reader could get the idea that the arguments given for the false side were effective enough to be capable of convincing, rather than being easy to refute." [44]

The preliminary section of the judges' sentence was still not finished. Their opinion went on to address the matter of the certificate from Cardinal Bellarmine that Galileo had kept for some seventeen years. This note did not mention any order for the scientist to refrain from teaching the heliocentric theory, the judges admitted. Yet the certificate still condemned Galileo. Bellarmine had clearly told the scientist that Copernicus's views contradicted Holy Scripture and Galileo had gone ahead and written a book championing these views, thereby showing his contempt for both Bellarmine and Scripture.

Finally, the man reading the sentence reached the section that listed Galileo's punishments:

> We say, pronounce, sentence and declare that you, Galileo, by reason of these things which have been detailed in the trial and which you have confessed already, have rendered yourself . . . vehemently suspect of heresy, namely of having held and believed a doctrine that is false and contrary to the divine and Holy Scripture, namely that [the] Sun is the center of the world and does not move from east to west, and that one may hold and defend as probable an opinion after it has been declared and defined contrary to Holy Scripture. . . . First, with a sincere heart and unfeigned faith, in our presence you [must] abjure, curse and detest the said errors and heresies, and every other error and heresy contrary to the Catholic and Apostolic Church in the manner and form we will prescribe to you. Furthermore, so that this grievous and pernicious error and transgression of yours may not go altogether unpunished, and so that you will be more cautious in future, and an example for others to abstain from delinquencies of this sort, we order that the book [the *Dialogue*] be prohibited by public edict. We condemn you to formal imprisonment in this Holy Office at our pleasure. As a salutary penance we impose on you to recite the seven penitential psalms once a week for the next three years.[45]

Preparing to Abjure

Fulfilling the pope's wish, Galileo had been sentenced to perform a public abjuration of his Copernican views. His book was to be banned and he was to suffer imprisonment for as long as the church saw fit. Immediately following the reading of the sentence, the judges stepped forward one by one and signed it as Galileo watched. It is an interesting footnote to history that only seven of them signed. The laws of the Roman Catholic Church did not

This seventeenth-century painting of Galileo's trial is completely fanciful. It depicts a jury and crowd of spectators, neither of which was actually involved.

require that the judges be unanimous in their decision. And despite the real risk of incurring the pope's wrath, three of the cardinals had the courage to abstain. One was Francesco Barberini, a moderate who admired Galileo and had often acted in his interests. The other two were Gaspare Borgia and Laudivio Zacchia.

Once the sentence had been signed, it was time for the condemned man to get down on his knees before the cardinals and other churchmen present and deliver his abjuration. Of all the punishments given to Galileo, this was the one he dreaded the most, mainly because of the intense shame and humiliation attached to the act. As Giorgio de Santillana explains, "The really serious point, which a modern [person] might fail to appreciate, was that of a solemn abjuration, which was a social dishonor and a brand of infamy in the Catholic society of the time."[46]

Moreover, the abjuration the cardinals demanded that Galileo read aloud included words that indicated that he had not been a good Catholic. Galileo found this particularly upsetting, since he considered himself a devout person. In his view, whatever errors he had made were motivated by his enthusiasm for science and were not intended to damage the Catholic faith. It also bothered Galileo that one clause in the prepared abjuration said that he had deviously misled the church censor in an effort to obtain permission to publish his book. To the contrary, Galileo felt that he had applied for permission from the Vatican in a straightforward manner. According to the diary of G.F. Buonamici, then a former secretary to the Tuscan ambassador in Rome, the scientist was very reluctant to say in his abjuration that he had been either a bad Catholic or a devious person:

> [Galileo] begged the cardinals that, if they insisted on proceeding against him in such a manner, they should at least leave out two points and then have him say whatever they pleased. The first one was that he should not be made to say that he was not a good Catholic, for he was and intended to remain one despite all his enemies could say. The other [was] that he would not say that he had ever deceived anybody, especially in the publishing of his book, which he had submitted in full candor to ecclesiastical censure [the church's censorship] and had it printed after legally obtaining a license [from the church].[47]

Evidently, the cardinals did not want to allow the proceedings to drag on and on with arguments about Galileo's two objections, which they viewed as fairly minor points. So they quietly conceded and allowed Galileo to omit them from his abjuration.

The Abjuration

It is perhaps a testimonial to Galileo's high degree of popularity, including among many churchmen, that he had successfully negotiated and altered some of the content of his abjuration. However, there was no way for him to escape the actual act of recanting his condemned beliefs. At a given signal, he knelt before the members of the court, placed his hand on a Bible, and gathered his courage as best as he could. "I, Galileo Galilei," he began, aged seventy years, arraigned personally before this tribunal, and kneeling before you, most Eminent and Reverend Lord Cardinals . . . [and] having before my eyes and touching with my hands, the Holy Gospels, swear that I have always believed, do now believe, and by God's help will for the future believe, all that is held, preached, and taught by the Holy Catholic and Apostolic Roman Church.

This was part of a traditional formula in which the person recanting reaffirmed his or her adherence and loyalty to the Bible and the Catholic Church. Next came a description of the specific crime of which Galileo had been accused and found guilty:

But whereas—after an injunction had been judicially intimated to me by this Holy Office, to the effect that I must altogether abandon the false opinion that the Sun is the center of the world and immovable, and that the Earth is not the center of the world, and moves, and that I must not hold, defend, or teach in any way whatsoever, verbally or in writing, the said doctrine, and after it had been notified to me that the said doctrine was contrary to Holy Scripture— I wrote and printed a book in which I discuss this doctrine already condemned, and adduce arguments of great cogency in its favor . . . and for this cause I have been pronounced by the Holy Office to be vehemently suspected of heresy.

Finally came the critical renunciation of "said doctrine," that is, the heliocentric view of the heavens:

Therefore, desiring to remove from the minds of your Eminences, and of all faithful Christians, this strong suspicion, reasonably conceived against me, with sincere heart and unfeigned faith I abjure, curse, and detest the aforesaid errors and heresies. . . . And I swear that in the future I will never again say or assert, verbally or in writing, anything that might furnish occasion for a similar suspicion regarding me.

Galileo went on to say that thereafter, if he ever had contact with a heretic, or even someone suspected of heresy, he would denounce that person to the Inquisition. He also promised that, if he himself ever said or did anything that could be construed as heresy, he would willingly accept any punishment the church deemed just and fitting. He ended his abjuration with the following words:

GALILEO'S DAUGHTER CONSOLES HIM

Galileo's daughter Virginia (Sister Maria Celeste) stayed in touch with him whenever he was away from Florence. This is part of a letter she wrote him (from Dava Sobel's translation of her letters) on July 2, 1633, after hearing about his sentence and abjuration.

A portrait of Sister Maria Celeste, Galileo's daughter.

Just as suddenly and unexpectedly as word of your new torment reached me, Sire, so intensely did it pierce my soul with pain to hear the judgment that has finally been passed, denouncing your person as harshly as your book. . . . Not having any letters from you this week, I could not calm myself, as though I already knew all that had happened. My dearest lord father, now is the time to avail yourself more than ever of that prudence which the Lord God has granted you, bearing these blows with that strength of spirit which your religion, your profession, and your age require. And since you, by virtue of your vast experience, can lay claim to full cognizance [understanding] of the fallacy and instability of everything in this miserable world, you must not make too much of these storms, but rather take hope that they will soon subside and transform themselves from troubles into as many satisfactions. . . . May it please God to see things turn out . . . for the best. Meanwhile, I pray you not to leave me without the consolation of your letters, giving me reports of your condition, physically and especially spiritually. Though I conclude my writing here, I never cease to accompany you with my thoughts and prayers, calling on His Divine Majesty to grant you true peace and consolation.

I, the said Galileo Galilei, have abjured, sworn, promised, and bound myself as above; and in witness of the truth thereof I have with my own hand subscribed the present document of my abjuration, and recited it word for word at Rome, in the Convent of Minerva, this twenty-second day of June, 1633.[48]

House Arrest

With the abjuration completed, Galileo's trial came to a close. Some churchmen escorted him out of the convent and led him toward a waiting carriage. Many modern books about the maverick scientist and his trial include the now famous anecdote in which, after stepping outside, he defiantly stamped his foot and shouted, "Yet the Earth *does* move!" This, however, is a myth, probably first introduced by an eighteenth-century admirer of Galileo (although some experts argue that he may have said it later, in private to sympathetic friends) It is part and parcel of the larger myth that he heroically stood up to his accusers and defended the Copernican theory. The sad reality was that Galileo was now an elderly, frail, careworn man who lacked the spirit and desire to fight the most powerful institution in Italian society—the Roman Catholic Church. So, he meekly submitted and recanted. Even the staunchest supporters of Galileo and Copernicus at the time realized that he simply had no other choice.

The carriage carried Galileo back to his quarters in the Tuscan embassy. The days he spent there marked the beginning of his imprisonment, which took the form of house arrest. His friend the Tuscan ambassador, Francesco Niccolini, went to the pope and begged him to pardon the scientist. Urban refused to grant a pardon. But he did agree to allow Galileo to be transferred to the custody of another friend, Archbishop Ascanio Piccolomini, in Siena. (Piccolomini had earlier invited Galileo to visit him at the conclusion of the trial.)

The relief that Galileo and his family and friends felt knowing that he would be treated well in captivity was reflected in a letter written to him by his daughter Virginia (now known as Sister Maria Celeste) on June 25, 1633:

FRANCESCO NICCOLINI

One of the key figures in Galileo's life during the trial was his friend Francesco Niccolini, the Tuscan ambassador to Rome. Niccolini was born in Tuscany in November 1584, which made him forty-eight at the time of the trial. As a boy, Niccolini prepared himself for the priesthood. But in 1618, following his father's death, he left the monastery and married. Thanks to the influence of his well-to-do family in the Tuscan court, Niccolini was able to secure the position of ambassador to Rome in 1621, a post in which he served for the next twenty-two years. During and immediately following Galileo's trial in 1633, Niccolini housed the scientist in a comfortable section of the embassy and saw to his daily needs. The ambassador also lobbied the pope on several occasions on Galileo's behalf. Niccolini survived his controversial friend and died in 1650 in Florence.

I am very pleased that you are going to Siena . . . partly because you will avoid contact with the contagion of the [bubonic] plague [which was afflicting parts of Italy at the time] . . . and also because, hearing how that the archbishop invited you with such insistence and kindness, I feel certain that you will enjoy much pleasure and contentment there. Well I pray you to proceed at your own convenience, and to afford yourself every possible comfort, since you have now had to travel in two extremes of temperature, and also to give me news of yourself whenever you can. [49]

On July 6, Galileo left Rome. Three days later he reached Siena and began the final, brief chapter of his eventful life.

Chapter 5

The Legacy of Galileo and His Trial

G ALILEO SURVIVED HIS ordeal with the Inquisition by less than nine years. However, the legacy of his writings and of his trial survived for centuries and have become part of the intellectual discourse of the modern world. Galileo's work formed an important foundation for later scientists like Isaac Newton, James MacLachlan points out:

> Beyond his telescopic discoveries, [Galileo] put experimental measurement at the heart of physics. And his mathematical insight moved physics out of windy philosophy and into real science. For 350 years Galileo's name has also evoked powerful social feelings. [Thanks to the events of his trial] in the first century after his death, Galileo symbolized the fight for freedom in science against the arrayed forces of philosophy and religion—against the traditions of Aristotle and the militancy of [conservative Catholic clergymen]. [50]

Indeed, whether or not the label of scientific martyr is justified by his actions before and during the trial, which remains a matter of dispute, that is how Galileo is still widely remembered. With the passage of time and the steady progression of science, the intellectual atmosphere in Europe changed drastically. And Galileo became enshrined in the growing pantheon of the heroes of science.

Galileo's Last Years

Not surprisingly, Galileo did not foresee any of this future hero worship in the years following his trial. When he arrived at Archbishop Piccolomini's house in Siena in early July 1633, the scientist was quite understandably exhausted and depressed from his long ordeal with the Inquisition. The cultured and gracious Piccolomini made it his mission to try to cheer up his friend. To this end, the churchman invited numerous educated people to visit and converse with the forlorn scientist. Over the course of some weeks, this did much to restore Galileo's spirit. And he soon resumed work on a book that he had begun in fits and starts two years before—the *Dialogues Concerning Two New Sciences.*

In the meantime, Galileo's other friends did not remain idle. On November 13, Ambassador Niccolini saw the pope again and asked that the scientist be allowed to return to his home. In Arcetri, near Florence and not far from the convent in which his daughters lived, Galileo had a small farm. Galileo could serve out his sentence on that farm just as well as at the archbishop's house, Niccolini argued. Pope Urban still harbored ill feelings toward Galileo, but at the beginning of December he relented and gave permission for the scientist to make the journey from Siena to Arcetri. (The conditions were that he must remain under house arrest and have few visitors.) On December 10, Maria Celeste wrote to her father: "We are awaiting your arrival with great longing, and we cheer ourselves to see how the weather has cleared for your journey."[51]

Only a few months later, Maria Celeste, who had been ill for some time, died. Filled with grief and now alone for long periods in his house on the farm, Galileo consoled himself by working on the *Two New Sciences.* Like the format of his earlier book, the *Dialogue*, it consisted of a conversation between three men—Salviati, Sagredo, and Simplicio—over the course of four days. This time, however, the topic was far less controversial. The new book, probably Galileo's greatest single contribution to modern science, deals with mechanics and the laws of motion. The work was published in the Netherlands in 1638. (Galileo's friends, who made the

arrangements, could not get it printed in Italy because all the pub-
lishers there feared getting in trouble with the church; the Netherlands, however, was a Protestant country and beyond the reach of
the Vatican.)

By the time the *Two New Sciences* was in print, Galileo was blind,
the victim of years of squinting through tiny, imperfect telescope

*The exterior of Galileo's house in Arcetri, near Florence. There, he spent his
last years in relative obscurity and gradually lost his vision.*

GALILEO MEASURES THE AIR

In this excerpt from his last great scientific work, the *Dialogues Concerning Two New Sciences* (Henry Crew's and Alfonso de Salvio's translation), Galileo explains how he proved that air has measurable weight.

I took a rather large glass bottle with a narrow neck and attached to it a leather cover, binding it tightly about the neck of the bottle. In the top of this cover, I inserted and firmly fastened the valve of a leather bottle, through which I forced into the glass bottle, by means of a syringe, a large quantity of air. . . . After this, I took an accurate balance [scale] and weighed this bottle of compressed air with the utmost precision, adjusting the weight with fine sand. I next opened the valve and allowed the compressed air to escape; then replaced the flask upon the balance and found it perceptibly lighter. From the sand which was used as a counterweight I now removed and laid aside as much as was necessary to again secure balance. Under these conditions, there can be no doubt but that the weight of the sand thus laid aside represents the weight of the air which had been forced into the flask and had afterwards escaped.

---

lenses. Out of compassion, the Duke of Tuscany sent a young mathematician to Arcetri to aid the afflicted scientist. Vincenzo Viviani, who would later write an important biography of Galileo, became his assistant, pupil, and faithful companion. Galileo died of a fever on January 8, 1642, at the age of seventy-seven. So close had he and his assistant become that when Viviani himself died in 1703, his remains were placed beside those of his mentor in Galileo's grave.

The Church's Black Eye

Well before Viviani's passing, the powerful legacy of Galileo's ideas and conflict with the church was already taking shape. In Italy, where the Inquisition was still strong, scientific activity and progress slowed, as many intellectuals feared suffering Galileo's fate. In contrast, in Protestant countries such as England and the Netherlands, scientific endeavors were increasingly encouraged. At the same time, in the 1600s the focus of economic power in Europe shifted away from Italy and the Mediterranean region to England, France, the Netherlands, and other Atlantic coastal areas. These lands heavily explored and colonized the Americas. And the spirit of discovery and increase in wealth that accompanied these events helped to promote the advance of science.

For these reasons, northern Europe became the center of the modern scientific revolution that had begun with men like Copernicus and Galileo. In 1655 Dutch physicist Christiaan Huygens built an improved version of Galileo's telescopes and discovered the rings of Saturn. Two years later, Huygens constructed a pendulum clock based on Galileo's work with pendulums. Meanwhile, only a year after Galileo's death, the great English scientist Isaac Newton was born. By 1665, Newton had invented the mathematical discipline of calculus. And in 1684, after making improvements

Isaac Newton, one of the greatest scientists of all time, was an intellectual heir of Galileo, whose ideas about motion Newton later refined.

in Galileo's rules of motion, he introduced the monumental theory of universal gravitation.

In the meantime, the rapid advance of science made it clear to all that Copernicus and Galileo had been right and the church had been wrong. The Sun was the center of the solar system after all. And Earth was just one of many planets that revolved around it, just as Galileo had been tried and punished for advocating.

This vindication of Galileo, along with the overly romanticized biographies of him by Viviani and others, transformed the great scientist into more of a hero than he really was. It also gave the Catholic Church a black eye that, fair or not, never quite healed properly. Most people oversimplified the confrontation between Galileo and the church as a fight between "enlightened thought" and "ignorance," or between "progress" and "backwardness." And this tended to promote the view that science and religion are somehow naturally incompatible and destined always to be at odds with each other. The reality, though, is that this need not be and often is not the case. Indeed, this was certainly not the case with Galileo himself, as Jerome Langford points out:

> Galileo was both a scientist and a believer; it was Galileo the scientist who wrote, Galileo the believer who recanted. But the lesson of his conflict with the church is not that science and faith are essentially opposed. The lesson lies rather in its dramatic verification of what disaster can come to science or faith when either of these is extended beyond its proper boundaries and enters the domain of the other. [52]

Over time, this lesson was taken more and more to heart by leading figures on both sides of the issue. Many scientists, like Galileo, remained religious but learned to reconcile the basic tenets of their beliefs with the continuing discoveries made by their chosen trade. Meanwhile, many religious leaders also came to see that biblical and scientific doctrines could be satisfactorily reconciled. Once again, Galileo provided the model. He had made the point that as long as the Scriptures were not taken too literally, one could accept the vision of a universe in which God created the natural laws that scientists later discovered and described.

A highly romanticized depiction of Galileo shows him absorbed in thought in preparation for one of his many experiments.

The Two Realms of Knowledge

Still, the fact is that the church as an institution was a good deal slower than many of its individual members in coming around to this more broad-minded, sophisticated viewpoint. Langford, himself a Catholic clergyman, admits:

> The Church's reaction to scientific advance has seemed to follow the same pattern for centuries. The scientific discovery of a theory is announced, and theologians react

defensively. The scientific evidence gains acceptance, and theologians begin to investigate ways of incorporating the new insights either by changing their interpretation of Scripture or by doing a bit of reorganizing of their pet world-views. Usually by the time theologians get around to accepting a scientific discovery, they are years behind the times.[53]

The tendency for the church to play catch-up in scientific matters was particularly evident in the cases of the heliocentric theory and Galileo. By 1700, all scientists, including those who were priests, accepted the fact that Earth revolves around the Sun. Yet it was not until 1822 that the Roman Catholic Church officially removed the 1616 prohibition against works dealing with the Copernican view of the heavens.

The church was even slower in admitting the error it had made in bringing Galileo to trial and then punishing him for advocating a theory that turned out to be correct. In July 1981, Pope John Paul II

In 1981 Pope John Paul II called for a church commission to review Galileo's case. The pope admitted that Galileo had been right.

POPE JOHN PAUL ADMITS THAT GALILEO WAS RIGHT

These are excerpts from the 1992 statement by Pope John Paul II (quoted in the journal *L'Osservatore Romano* on November 4 of that year) in which he admitted that the Catholic Church was wrong to condemn Galileo.

> From the Galileo affair, we can learn a lesson which remains valid in relation to similar situations which occur today and which may occur in the future. In Galileo's time, to depict the world as lacking an absolute physical reference point was, so to speak, inconceivable. And since the cosmos, as it was then known, was contained within the solar system alone, this reference point could only be situated in the Earth or in the Sun. Today . . . neither of these two reference points has the importance they once had. This observation . . . [shows] that often, beyond two partial and contrasting perceptions, there exists a wider perception which includes them and goes beyond both of them. Another lesson which we can draw is that the different branches of knowledge call for different methods. Thanks to his intuition as a brilliant physicist . . . Galileo, who practically invented the experimental method, understood why only the Sun could function as the center of the world, as it was then known. . . . The error of the theologians of the time, when they maintained the centrality of the Earth, was to think that our understanding of the physical world's structure was, in some way, imposed by the literal sense of Sacred Scripture. . . . In fact, the Bible does not concern itself with the details of the physical world, the understanding of which is the competence of human experience and reasoning. There exist two realms of knowledge, one which has its source in Revelation and one which reason can discover by its own power. . . . The two realms are not altogether foreign to each other, they have points of contact. The methodologies proper to each make it possible to bring out different aspects of reality. . . . The scientist who is conscious of this twofold development and takes it into account contributes to the restoration of harmony.

established a special commission of ecclesiastical scholars to study the Galileo case. Eleven years later, on October 31, 1992, the commission gave the pope its report and he formally conceded that back in the 1600s the church had been wrong. The mistake made by the religious authorities at the time, he said, was interpreting the Scriptures too literally, which led to an unfortunate rejection of the reality of the heliocentric system. "The problem posed by theologians of that age," John Paul stated, was

> the compatibility between heliocentrism and Scripture. Thus the new science, with its methods and the freedom of research which they implied, obliged theologians to examine their own criteria of scriptural interpretation. Most of them did not know how to do so. Paradoxically, Galileo, a sincere believer, showed himself to be more perceptive in this regard than the theologians who opposed him. "If Scripture cannot err," he wrote to Benedetto Castelli, "certain of its interpreters and commentators can and do so in many ways." . . . The majority of theologians did not recognize the formal distinction between Sacred Scripture and its interpretation, and this led them unduly to transpose into the realm of the doctrine of the faith a question which in fact pertained to scientific investigation. [54]

John Paul also recognized that it is important for future churchmen and scientists not to make the same mistakes that occurred in the Galileo affair. The way to avoid confrontations between science and faith, he said, is to accept that they are two distinct disciplines. Although they sometimes come together at "points of contact," they should for the most part remain separate, respect each other's space, and thereby both be viable and meaningful:

> From the Galileo affair we can learn a lesson which remains valid in relation to similar situations which occur today and which may occur in the future. . . . Different branches of knowledge call for different methods. . . . There exist two realms of knowledge, one which has its source in Revelation [one of the Scriptures] and one which reason can discover by its own power. To the latter belong especially the experimental sciences and philosophy. The distinction between the two realms of knowledge ought not to be understood as opposition. The

two realms are not altogether foreign to each other, they have points of contact. The methodologies proper to each make it possible to bring out different aspects of reality.[55]

At the core of the pope's message seems to rest the hope that the two realms of knowledge—one rooted in the material world, the other in the spiritual one—can hereafter coexist in harmony. If they can, Galileo's tragic showdown with the church will not have been in vain.

Notes

Introduction: When Religion and Science Work at Cross-Purposes

1. Galileo Galilei, *Le Opere di Galileo Galilei*, ed. Antonio Favaro, 20 vols. Florence, Italy: G. Barbera Editrice, 1968, vol. 19, p. 406.

2. Jerome J. Langford, *Galileo, Science, and the Church*. Ann Arbor: University of Michigan Press, 1992, p. xiii.

3. Richard Blackwell, "Could There Be Another Galileo Case?" in Peter Machamer, ed., *The Cambridge Companion to Galileo*. Cambridge, England: Cambridge University Press, 1998, p. 348.

4. Charles Van Doren, *A History of Knowledge: Past, Present, and Future*. New York: Ballantine, 1991, p. 201.

5. Quoted in Michael Segre, "The Never-Ending Galileo Story," in Machamer, *Cambridge Companion to Galileo*, p. 395.

6. Langford, *Galileo*, p. 160.

Chapter 1: An Outspoken Thinker in an Age of Change

7. Langford, *Galileo*, p. 2.

8. Langford, *Galileo*, p. 2.

9. James MacLachlan, *Galileo Galilei: First Physicist*. New York: Oxford University Press, 1997, p. 21.

10. Quoted in Morris R. Cohen and I.E. Drabkin, eds., *A Source Book in Greek Science*. Cambridge, MA: Harvard University Press, 1948, p. 148.

11. Nicholas Copernicus, *On the Revolutions*, trans. Edward Rosen. Baltimore, MD: Johns Hopkins University Press, 1992, p. 38.

12. Quoted in Galilei, *Le Opere di Galileo*, vol. 10, p. 68.

13. Giordano Bruno, *The Ash Wednesday Supper*, trans. Stanley L. Jaki. Dartmouth College, 1999, p. 7. http://hilbert.dartmouth.edu/~matc/Readers/renaissance.astro/6.1.Supper.html.

14. MacLachlan, *Galileo*, p. 50.

15. Quoted in Giorgio de Santillana, *The Crime of Galileo*. Chicago: University of Chicago Press, 1955, p. 9.

Chapter 2: The New Astronomy vs. the Holy Scriptures

16. Ecclesiastes 1.5.

17. Psalms 92.1.
18. Quoted in Galilei, *Le Opere di Galileo Galilei*, vol. 5, pp. 281–84.
19. Quoted in Galilei, *Le Opere di Galileo Galilei*, vol. 5, pp. 285–86.
20. Langford, *Galileo*, p. 55.
21. Quoted in Stillman Drake, *Galileo at Work: His Scientific Biography*. Chicago: University of Chicago Press, 1978, p. 239.
22. Quoted in Galilei, *Le Opere di Galileo Galilei*, vol. 12, p. 129.
23. Quoted in Santillana, *The Crime of Galileo*, p. 46. It must be noted that some modern scholars doubt that Lorini was the culprit who altered the letter. In fact, it is possible that the copy that came into his possession had already been altered by someone hostile to Galileo.
24. Quoted in Galilei, *Le Opere di Galileo Galilei*, vol. 12, pp. 171–72.
25. Quoted in Galilei, *Le Opere di Galileo Galilei*, vol. 12, pp. 226–27.
26. Quoted in Galilei, *Le Opere di Galileo Galilei*, vol. 19, pp. 321–22.
27. Quoted in Galilei, *Le Opere di Galileo Galilei*, vol. 11, p. 216.
28. Langford, *Galileo*, p. 114.

Chapter 3: Galileo on Trial: The Initial Depositions

29. Galileo Galilei, *Dialogue Concerning the Two Chief World Systems*, trans. Stillman Drake. Berkeley: University of California Press, 1967, pp. 319, 321.
30. Quoted in Galilei, *Le Opere di Galileo Galilei*, vol. 19, pp. 336–37.
31. Quoted in Galilei, *Le Opere di Galileo Galilei*, vol. 19, pp. 337–38.
32. Quoted in Galilei, *Le Opere di Galileo Galilei*, vol. 19, pp. 338–40.
33. Quoted in Galilei, *Le Opere di Galileo Galilei*, vol. 15, p. 107.
34. Quoted in Galilei, *Le Opere di Galileo Galilei*, vol. 19, p. 342.
35. Quoted in Galilei, *Le Opere di Galileo Galilei*, vol. 19, p. 343.
36. Quoted in Galilei, *Le Opere di Galileo Galilei*, vol. 19, p. 344.
37. Quoted in "Galileo's Defense and Depositions," in Douglas Linder, "The Trial of Galileo," 2002. www.law.umkc.edu/faculty/projects/ftrials/galileo/galileo.html.
38. Quoted in "Galileo's Defense and Depositions."
39. Quoted in Galilei, *Le Opere di Galileo Galilei*, vol. 19, pp. 360–61.

Chapter 4: Galileo on Trial: The Sentence and Abjuration

40. Quoted in Galilei, *Le Opere di Galileo Galilei*, vol. 19, p. 361.

41. Quoted in Galilei, *Le Opere di Galileo Galilei,* vol. 19, p. 362.
42. Quoted in Galilei, *Le Opere di Galileo Galilei,* vol. 19, p. 405.
43. Quoted in Galilei, *Le Opere di Galileo Galilei,* vol. 19, p. 405.
44. Quoted in Galilei, *Le Opere di Galileo Galilei,* vol. 19, p. 406.
45. Quoted in Galilei, *Le Opere di Galileo Galilei,* vol. 19, p. 406.
46. Santillana, *The Crime of Galileo,* p. 248.
47. Quoted in Santillana, *The Crime of Galileo,* p. 311.
48. Quoted in Galilei, *Le Opere di Galileo Galilei,* vol. 19, p. 406.
49. Quoted in Dava Sobel, trans., Letters of Maria Celeste, in "Galileo's Daughter," 1999. http://es.rice.edu/ES/humsoc/Galileo/MariaCeleste.

Chapter 5: The Legacy of Galileo and His Trial
50. MacLachlan, *Galileo,* p. 109.
51. Quoted in Sobel, "Galileo's Daughter."
52. Langford, *Galileo,* p. 180.
53. Langford, *Galileo,* p. 185.
54. Quoted in *L'Osservatore Romano,* November 4, 1992, p. 3.
55. Quoted in *L'Osservatore Romano,* p. 4.

Timeline

1543

Polish astronomer Nicolaus Copernicus publishes *On the Revolutions*, in which he describes a heliocentric vision of the heavens similar to that first proposed in ancient Greece.

1564

Galileo is born in Pisa, in the Italian state of Tuscany.

1574

Galileo enters the school of a monastery near Florence, also in Tuscany.

1585

Italian scholar and former monk Giordano Bruno publishes *The Ash Wednesday Supper*, in which he claims that the stars are other suns, each having planets inhabited by people.

1589

Galileo becomes a teacher of mathematics at the University of Pisa.

1592

Galileo begins teaching at the University of Padua, in the Republic of Venice.

1600

The Inquisition, an arm of the Roman Catholic Church, burns Giordano Bruno at the stake for refusing to recant his revolutionary views about the heavens.

1609

Galileo builds a telescope and observes the Moon, on which he sees craters and mountains.

1610

Galileo discovers the four largest moons of Jupiter, proving that Earth is not the only body around which celestial objects revolve; he publishes his telescopic discoveries to date in the *Starry Messenger*.

1613

Galileo publishes *Letters on Sunspots*, in which he asserts that the Sun's surface is marred by dark splotches.

1616

Copernicus's book, along with others advocating the heliocentric view of the heavens, is prohibited by the church; a leading church-man warns Galileo that the heliocentric theory does not conform to statements in the Scriptures.

1624

Galileo visits Rome and meets with Pope Urban VIII six times; the pope gives the scientist the impression that it is all right to discuss the Copernican view as long as it is labeled a hypothesis.

1629

Galileo finishes the initial draft of the *Dialogue Concerning the Two Chief World Systems*, a thinly veiled endorsement of the heliocentric view.

1632

After being cleared by the church's censor, the *Dialogue* is published.

1633

After he angers the pope, Galileo is tried by the Inquisition on sus-picion of heresy, is forced to renounce the heliocentric view, and begins to serve an indefinite term of house arrest.

1638

Galileo's book about the laws of motion—the *Dialogues Concerning Two New Sciences*—is published in the Netherlands.

1642

Still under house arrest, Galileo dies on his farm near Florence.

1717

The first and most influential major biography of Galileo, by his for-mer pupil and friend Vincenzo Viviani, is published posthumously.

1822

The Catholic Church lifts its prohibition of works advocating the heliocentric view.

1992

A commission of scholars appointed by Pope John Paul II delivers the results of its study of the Galileo affair; the pope admits that Galileo was right and the church was wrong.

For Further Reading

Books

Catherine M. Adronik, *Copernicus: Founder of Modern Astronomy*. Berkeley Heights, NJ: Enslow, 2002. Excellent basic overview of Copernicus and his formulation of the heliocentric theory, which inspired Galileo.

Mike Goldsmith, *Galileo Galilei*. New York: Raintree/Steck Vaughn, 2002. One of the better presentations for young readers of Galileo's contributions to science.

Paul Mason, *Galileo*. Chicago: Heinemann Library, 2001. A colorfully illustrated overview of Galileo's life and work.

Michael White, *Galileo Galilei: Inventor, Astronomer, and Rebel*. San Diego: Blackbirch, 1999. Well-written introductory account of Galileo's achievements for young readers.

Internet Sources

Alwyn Botha, "Galileo Galilei," 2002. www.galileo-galilei.org. A series of entertaining and informative quizzes about Galileo's life, inventions, and writings.

Lucid Interactive, "Galileo Galilei: Astronomer and Physicist," 2003. www.lucidcafe.com/library/96feb/galileo.html. A useful brief overview of Galileo's contributions, supplemented by numerous links to related sites.

———, "Nicolaus Copernicus: Cleric and Astronomer," 2003. www.lucidcafe.com/library/96feb/copernicus.html. Short but informative synopsis of Copernicus's ideas and writings, supplemented by many links to related sites.

Works Consulted

Major Works

Primary Sources

Giordano Bruno, *The Ash Wednesday Supper.* Trans. Stanley L. Jaki. Dartmouth College, 1999. http://hilbert.dartmouth.edu/~matc/Readers/renaissance.astro/6.1.Supper.html. One of the two major astronomical works of Galileo's important contemporary Bruno, whom the church burned at the stake.

Morris R. Cohen and I.E. Drabkin, eds., *A Source Book in Greek Science.* Cambridge, MA: Harvard University Press, 1948. One of the leading standard collections of translations of ancient Greek scientific works.

Nicholas Copernicus, *On the Revolutions.* Trans. Edward Rosen. Baltimore, MD: Johns Hopkins University Press, 1992. The groundbreaking work advocating the Sun-centered universe, which greatly inspired Galileo and was eventually banned by the church.

Stillman Drake, ed., *Discoveries and Opinions of Galileo.* Garden City, NY: Doubleday, 1957. A useful compilation of translations of several of Galileo's chief writings.

Galileo Galilei, *Dialogue Concerning the Two Chief World Systems.* Trans. Stillman Drake. Berkeley: University of California Press, 1967. Galileo's controversial work that brought him into conflict with the church.

———, *Dialogues Concerning Two New Sciences.* Trans. Henry Crew and Alfonso de Salvio. Buffalo, NY: Prometheus, 1991. The important scientific work that Galileo wrote while under house arrest following his trial.

———, *Le Opere di Galileo Galilei.* Ed. Antonio Favaro. 20 vols. Florence, Italy: G. Barbera Editrice, 1968. The most comprehensive and most widely used collection of primary-source documents by and about Galileo.

Douglas Linder, "The Trial of Galileo," 2002. www.law.umkc.edu/faculty/projects/ftrials/galileo/galileo.html. A useful collection of some of the main documents associated with Galileo's confrontation with the Inquisition.

Dava Sobel, trans., Letters of Maria Celeste, in "Galileo's Daughter," 1999. http://es.rice.edu/ES/humsoc/Galileo/MariaCeleste. A collection of English translations of the 124 letters written to Galileo by his daughter Virginia (Sister Maria Celeste).

Modern Sources

Stillman Drake, *Galileo at Work: His Scientific Biography*. Chicago: University of Chicago Press, 1978. A monumental study of Galileo's scientific endeavors by the leading Galileo scholar of the twentieth century.

Jerome J. Langford, *Galileo, Science, and the Church*. Ann Arbor: University of Michigan Press, 1992. A superior study of Galileo's intellectual differences with the church, culminating in his trial.

L'Osservatore Romano, November 4, 1992. Contains an English translation of Pope John Paul II's 1992 exoneration of Galileo.

Peter Machamer, ed., *The Cambridge Companion to Galileo*. Cambridge, England: Cambridge University Press, 1998. An excellent, up-to-date collection of essays about Galileo's life and work by leading scholars.

James MacLachlan, *Galileo Galilei: First Physicist*. New York: Oxford University Press, 1997. A brief but well-written and informative look at Galileo's scientific discoveries and trial.

Giorgio de Santillana, *The Crime of Galileo*. Chicago: University of Chicago Press, 1955. An important, sometimes controversial modern study of Galileo's run-in with the church.

Selected Additional Works

Angus Armitage, *The World of Copernicus*. New York: Mentor, 1961.

Richard J. Blackwell, *Galileo, Bellarmine, and the Church*. South Bend, IN: University of Notre Dame Press, 1991.

James S.J. Brodrick, *Galileo*. New York: Harper and Row, 1965.

Stillman Drake, *Galileo*. New York: Oxford University Press, 1980.

Annibale Fantoli, *Galileo: For Copernicanism and for the Church*. Vatican City: Vatican Observatory, 1994.

Hilary Gatti, *Giordano Bruno and the Renaissance Science*. Ithaca, NY: Cornell University Press, 2002.

Thomas S. Kuhn, *The Copernican Revolution: Planetary Astronomy in the Development of Western Thought*. New York: Random House, 1959.

William R. Shea, *Galileo's Intellectual Revolution*. New York: Science History, 1972.

Alan G.R. Smith, *Science and Society in the Sixteenth and Seventeenth Centuries*. London: Thames and Hudson, 1972.

Charles Van Doren, *A History of Knowledge: Past, Present, and Future*. New York: Ballantine, 1991.

Index

Picture Credits

About the Author

In addition to his acclaimed volumes on the ancient world, historian Don Nardo has produced several studies of medieval times, including *Life on a Medieval Pilgrimage*, *The Medieval Castle*, and *The Black Death*. In addition to this book on the trial of Galileo, he has also published a study of another famous medieval trial—that of Joan of Arc. Mr. Nardo resides with his wife, Christine, in Massachusetts.